SIZZLING
SEASONAL
SCRAPBOOK PAGES

The Noto Family

MEMORY
MAKERS
BOOKS

Executive Editor Kerry Arquette   **Founder** Michele Gerbrandt

Editor Shannon Hurd
Art Director Andrea Zocchi
Designer Nick Nyffeler
Craft Editor Jodi Amidei
Idea Editor Janetta Wieneke
Photographer Ken Trujillo
Contributing Photographers Marc Creedon, Lois Duncan, Brenda Martinez, Ron Nichols
Contributing Writers Kelly Angard, Lois Duncan, Ron Nichols
Editorial Support MaryJo Regier, Dena Twinem

Published by Memory Makers Books, an imprint of F & W Publications, Inc.
12365 Huron Street, Suite 500, Denver, CO 80234
Phone 1-800-254-9124

First edition. Printed in Singapore

07 06 05 04 03 5 4 3 2

Library of Congress Cataloging-in-Publication Data

Sizzling seasonal scrapbook pages
    p. cm.
    Includes bibliographical references.
    ISBN 1-892127-28-8
    1. Photograph albums. 2. Photographs--Conservation and restoration. 3. Scrapbooks. I.
Memory Makers Books.

TR465.S59 2003
745.593--dc21

2003050991

Distributed to trade and art markets by
F & W Publications, Inc.
4700 East Galbraith Road, Cincinnati, OH 45236
Phone 1-800-289-0963

ISBN 1-892127-28-8

Memory Makers Books is the home of *Memory Makers*, the scrapbook magazine dedicated to educating and inspiring scrapbookers.
To subscribe, or for more information, call 1-800-366-6465.
Visit us on the Internet at www.memorymakersmagazine.com

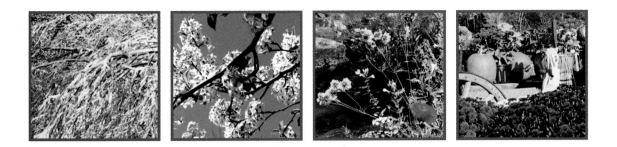

ALBUM OF THE HEART

by Lois Duncan

As the year draws to an end
We grow close again,
Turning pages of our lives,
Pausing now and then

To recall a magic time
Or a special place.
Springtime sunlight leaps at us
From a smiling face.

Summer laughter rings anew,
Mixed with autumn tears.
Seasons blend and mesh and blur,
With the flying years.

Guard the album of the heart.
There the memories are—
Gentle as the drifting snow
Holy as the star.

TABLE OF CONTENTS

Just hear those sleigh bells jingling...

December 2001 in Breckenridge, Colorado...the perfect time of year for a real sleigh ride. None of us had ever ridden in a horse-drawn sleigh before. The weather was perfect... crisp, cold air with tiny snowflakes gently falling all around. My niece Amanda had a wonderful time too, she stayed all snugly beneath all the blankets.

SNOW

Introduction

I've always loved the changing seasons: brilliant summer sunshine, colorful fall leaves, fragrant spring blossoms and winter's magical snow. The rotation of seasons offers more than just changing landscape—it allows people to break free from the comfort of their traditional cycles and experience new adventures.

The changing seasons also supply scrapbookers with an evolving panorama of wonderful memories to capture. One of my favorite seasonal memories involves a Christmas family sleigh ride in Breckenridge, Colorado. It was such a picture-perfect winter day, with the cold, crisp flurries falling delicately around our bundled-up bodies. Times like these just beg to be captured and preserved within our scrapbooks.

You undoubtedly have your own unique seasonal memories that are just waiting to find a home within your scrapbook album. This book, *Sizzling Seasonal Scrapbook Pages*, was created to supply you with the inspiration and information necessary to make each scrapbook page as cherished as the event or events it represents.

Inside, you'll find dozens of stunning scrapbook pages that highlight many of your favorite seasonal activities, including Super Bowl parties, backyard barbecues, graduation ceremonies, ski trips and, every child's favorite, back-to-school preparations!

The book also includes a plethora of creative, cutting-edge scrapbook techniques, as well as comprehensive photo lists that detail the most common seasonal events and activities your camera won't want to miss. As well, enjoy a special "photo tips" section, designed to help you meet season-specific photography challenges, such as how to create better composition, get rid of red-eye and capture those unexpected moments.

Every scrapbooker has her own favorite season and oodles of unique memories to go along with it. Whether you're a cold-weather fan, a budding spring lover or feel most connected to fall or summer, there's bound to be pages somewhere inside this book to inspire you.

Michele

Michele Gerbrandt
Founding Editor
Memory Makers magazine

Getting Started

Just like the seasons, the scrapbook market changes constantly. Dozens of new embellishments and accessories are created to help scrapbookers add creativity and pizazz to their pages. However, the basics of scrapbooking—the tools, the organization and the elements of a good layout—remain the same. Here's how to get started in a few easy steps.

1. Set Up a Work Area and Get Organized

Customize a well-lit, roomy work surface with access to photos, scrapbook supplies and idea books. Organize your photos into categories. Jot down memories on sticky notes as you go along. Group photos chronologically, by season or by holiday. Make sure to store photos and negatives in archival-quality binders, boxes or sleeves.

2. Basic Tools and Supplies

- Adhesives: Use "acid-free" or "photo safe" adhesives such as glues, tapes and mounting corners. Rubber cement, white school glue and cellophane tape contain chemicals that can harm photos over time.

- Papers: Acid- and lignin-free papers in a variety of patterns and textures are available in countless colors. Use these versatile papers for a background, an accent and to mat or frame photos.

- Albums: The quantity, physical size and theme of your photos will help determine what type of album you need. Albums come in three-ring binder, post-bound or strap-hinge style, allowing you to remove, add or rearrange pages as needed. Spiral-bound albums make great gifts.

- Design Additions and Embellishments: Elements such as stickers, die cuts, photo corners and pre-made embellishments can enhance the look of your page by building on the theme of your photos.

- Scissors and Paper Trimmer: A pair of sharp, straight-edge scissors and a paper trimmer are absolute necessities for photo cropping. Decorative scissors can add pizazz to a photo, matting or border element.

- Pencils, Pens and Markers: A rainbow of journaling pens and markers, with a variety of tips, make journaling and penmanship a snap. Photo-safe colored pencils can add colorful details to backgrounds and designs while wax pencils can be used for writing on the front or back of photos.

- Rulers and Templates: Decorative rulers and templates are the perfect accessory to crop photos or trace shapes onto paper, to cut decorative photo mats, or to create your own die cuts.

3. Create a Layout

- Focal Point: Select one photo for a focal point on the page; choose an enlarged, matted, unique or exceptional photo to draw the eye to the page.

- Balance: Make sure not to cluster too many photos in one area; leave space for journaling as well as room around the focal photo.

- Color: Select paper colors and patterns that don't distract from your photos.

4. Crop-n-Assemble

- Cropping: Photo cropping can add style, emphasize a subject or remove a busy background.

- Matting: Single or layered paper photo mats focus attention and add a finished touch to a photo.

5. Journaling

- Bullets: List the basics of who, what, when, where and why in bullet form.

- Captions: Expand information with complete sentences.

- Quotes, Poems and Sayings: Search out or write your own words pertaining to photo subject.

- Storytelling: Tell the story with creativity, just make sure to include the details!

6. The Complete Page

Enjoy the process and keep the focus on scrapbook fun and the preservation of your memories. Try not to get overwhelmed with the number of scrapbook products available. Be sure to let your own style come through!

How to take great photos

Every sizzling seasonal scrapbook page begins with sensational photographs. Whether those images are of people, places or things, good photographs are the result of careful composition, attention to lighting, and tenacity. The seasons, however, pose unique challenges that can hinder even the best of photographic endeavors. Fortunately, for every problem, there is a solution.

PROBLEM: Inside flashes produce red-eye and background shadows. **SOLUTION:** Try using higher-speed film (ASA 400) while standing next to a window or other natural light source.

PROBLEM: Shooting pictures on snow causes subjects to be underexposed (dark). **SOLUTION:** If using a camera with manual or programmable exposure controls (i.e. shutter and aperture control) overexpose the scene by one stop. If your camera doesn't have programmable exposure control, use your camera's flash to properly expose the subject.

PROBLEM: Pictures that tend to look the same. **SOLUTION:** Shoot vertical, as well as horizontal, photos. Experiment with different focal lengths to gain new perspectives.

PROBLEM: Composition seems static and uninteresting. **SOLUTION:** Avoid placing your subject in the center of the frame. Instead, try placing it offside to create visual balance.

PROBLEM: It's difficult to capture those wonderful spontaneous moments of children on film. **SOLUTION:** Keep your camera loaded with fresh batteries, film and in a readily accessible location (such as on the top of the refrigerator) at all times.

PROBLEM: To fill up the frame with the subject, you have to get close, and that affects the spontaneity of the moment. **SOLUTION:** Use a telephoto lens, which will allow you to obtain closer shots while standing farther away.

PROBLEM: Shooting during the mid-day hours creates flat colors and harsh shadows. **SOLUTION:** Shoot on over-cast days and during the "golden hours" (an hour before sunset or an hour after sun rise). If you must shoot midday, try taking your subjects into the shade.

PROBLEM: Pictures that are often "busy" and uninteresting. **SOLUTION:** Try focusing on "the little picture" as well as the scenic vistas. Look up, down and all around for unusual angles or subjects that tell your story.

WINTER

by Lois Duncan

What is springtime? Nothing now.
Ice-clad creeks are gray and still.
Snow is heaped in crusted drifts
In the woods and on the hill.

Branches stretch toward leaden skies,
Heartbreak-heavy, black and old.
Trees that have forgotten spring
Shiver, silent in the cold.

What is springtime? Nothing now.
Still, there is the faintest sound
Whispering beneath the earth—
Laughter deep in frozen ground.

January 2002

Every time you come into a room,
Every time I look at your sweet face,
Every time you give me a hug, every time I see you,
Every morning, every afternoon, every evening,
You fill my heart with love.

— Anon

Aysha

Trudy's sentimental layout and heartwarming poem is bordered with vellum snowflakes layered over touchably soft fiber strands. Print poem onto white cardstock, leaving room for photo; cut cardstock to size and mount photo. Freehand write title on white cardstock strip; paper tear left edge. Layer title block and photo with poem on light blue vellum (Paper Company) with paper-torn edges. Mount white and blue fiber strands (On The Surface, DMC) horizontally along top and bottom of page; wrap ends around back of page and secure. Mount vellum snowflake stickers (Autumn Leaves) over fibers. Mat page on blue vellum.

Trudy Sigurdson, Victoria, British Columbia, Canada

"Life isn't a matter of milestones, but of moments."
Rose Kennedy

Cheyenne is such a precious child, she really does make every moment special. I just love how these pictures capture some of her sweetness. 02/11/02

Winter Wonders

Brooke's patience and love for using a craft knife is evident when looking at her intricately detailed snowflakes. Download snowflake patterns from Internet clip art. Transfer patterns onto silver sparkled cardstock (Bazzill); carefully cut and detail with a craft knife. Alter some of the snowflake patterns slightly so that no two snowflakes look exactly alike. Single and double mat photos; overlap matting for photos on the right. Print journaling onto silver sparkle cardstock leaving space for matted photo. Print title; silhouette cut with craft knife.

Brooke Smith, Anchorage, Alaska

Winter Bliss

Dangling title letters sparkle just like fallen snow on Trudy's soothing, monochromatic page. Mat light purple cardstock with darker purple cardstock. Slice a 2½" strip of white cardstock; paper tear horizontally along one edge. Create title letters as illustrated below. Punch snowflakes (Emagination Crafts) from four different shades of purple cardstock; run through adhesive application machine before coating with glitter, as seen below. Mount on white 1¼" punched square with self-adhesive foam spacers. Mat on 1½" punched squares. Layer four matted snowflakes over fiber strands. Double mat photos; layer on page with remaining matted snowflakes. Print journaling on white cardstock; cut to size, mat and mount with self-adhesive foam spacers.

Trudy Sigurdson, Victoria, British Columbia, Canada

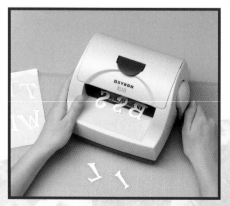

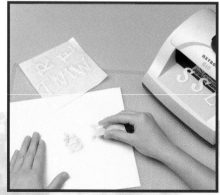

1 Using a Sizzix Die Cut Machine, cut out letters and run them through a adhesive application machine upside down.

2 Cover all letters with purplish-silver glitter, then run the letters glitter side up through the adhesive application machine again.

3 Mat letters on lavender cardstock. Punch 1⁄16" hole at the top of each letter and set aside. Tear two white strips of cardstock.

WINTER PHOTO CHECKLIST

- ❑ Christmas shopping
- ❑ Holiday decorating
- ❑ Cooking holiday meals
- ❑ First snow
- ❑ Family gatherings
- ❑ Snow sports (boarding/skiing/sledding/tubing)
- ❑ Snowman building, snowball fights, snow shoveling
- ❑ Ice-skating
- ❑ Winter dances
- ❑ Holiday parades
- ❑ Basketball games
- ❑ Hockey games/Stanley Cup
- ❑ Super Bowl parties
- ❑ College bowl games
- ❑ Christmas Eve/Day
- ❑ New Year's Eve/Day
- ❑ Hanukkah
- ❑ Kwanzaa
- ❑ Valentine's Day

Ski

Kelli gives a unique textured twist to punched and die-cut shapes by embossing with ultra thick embossing enamel (Ranger). Punch snowflakes (All Night Media, Emagination Crafts) and die cut title letters from thick, double-sided tape (Suze Weinberg). Sprinkle with embossing enamel and heat from underside until bubbly. Layer letters and snowflakes over paper-torn strip adorned with sheer ribbon strips and nailheads. Double mat large photo; cut thin strips of tape and emboss for matting trim. Mat smaller photos on red cardstock; tear all paper edges.

Kelli Noto, Centennial, Colorado

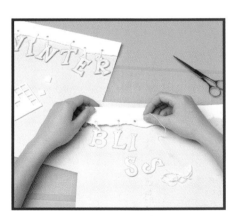

4 Punch holes in white cardstock strips and set eyelets. Hang letters from eyelets with fibers. Mount strips to page, attaching individual letters to page using self-adhesive foam spacers.

Alex HATES to skate. So imagine my surprise when he wanted to go on his Grade 1 field trip to Panorama Rec Center to go ice skating.

I should, however, have known better. He went once around the rink & then just MAD to get off the ice. Luckily I had someone take these pictures at the half way mark around the rink. When he got off, one of the teachers watched him & I stayed on to help the kids that needed it. OK, I'll be honest, I love to skate & didn't want to get off yet. At least one of us had fun! 1/25/01

Ice Skating

Ice skating is a hot cool-weather activity for young and old alike. Trudy cleverly recreated the graphic lines of the skating rink featured in her photos by layering sliced strips of vellum and cardstock. Experiment with various patterns before adhering pieces. To create the scoreboard title block punch $\frac{1}{8}$" circles from vellum. Arrange circles to form letters and numbers. Mount on multi-colored cardstock scoreboard blocks. Print journaling onto vellum; cut to size and mount. Mat photos on red cardstock and mount at skewed angles.

Trudy Sigurdson, Victoria, British Columbia, Canada

Speed

Gayla's colorful 12-photo kaleidoscope conveys motion and high-speed excitement. Create kaleidoscope with easy angle template (This n' That Crafts); assemble and mount over patterned paper (Creative Imaginations). Cut two 6" wide strips of light blue paper; mount at outsides of each page. Layer enlarged and cropped photos down left side of page. Mount one enlarged photo on right side of other page. Adhere title sticker letters (Creative Imaginations) under large photo. Print journaling on vellum; cut to size and mount with eyelets. Complete page with shaved ice glitter (Magic Scraps) around kaleidoscope and on side borders.

Gayla Feachen, Irving, Texas

..Speed

When we were at the snow tubing park Chelsea spotted the mini Ski-Doos and asked to drive one. It think she's going to be hell on wheels when she gets her license! January 1, 2002

Better than ice cream!

I found these tiny, faded, old photographs in an old album. I enhanced them to the best of my ability. They are of Jack and Barbara Petrick and their dog, Bingy, playing in the snow at their home in Plainfield, Wisconsin during the winters of 1940 and 1941.

Winter

Barbara's simple embellishments give her page clean lines and provide a beautiful contrast for old black-and-white photos. Mat patterned paper (Provo Craft) with black cardstock. Single and double mat photos; tear edges of second matting. Print journaling and title letters on white cardstock. Mat journaling; silhouette cut title letters. Tear white cardstock for title block; brush with black chalk around the edges. Silhouette computer-printed clip art of clothesline and mittens (Provo Craft) and snowman (Broderbund). Mount clothesline and mittens on torn title block; layer silhouette cut title letters on mittens. Mount snowman at right side of journaling block.

Barbara Gardener, Scottsdale, Arizona

Snow

Dry-embossed shapes etched into vellum add elegant, transparent effects to Torrey's color-blocked layout. Divide page into quadrants; cut cardstock in shades of blue with decorative scissors. Print poem. Mount quadrant pieces on light blue cardstock, leaving a ⅛" border. Cut vellum block for border and title with decorative scissors (Fiskars). Create title letters, feathers and snowflake designs as shown in instructions below, using pattern on page 93 or sketching freehand. Mount vellum with embossed side toward page. Double mat photo; trim with decorative scissors.

Torrey Miller, Thornton, Colorado
Photo, Heidi Finger, Brighton, Colorado

High above.
on clouds' soft bed.
the angels shake their wings...

to shed the shroud
of wint'ry sleep
that peaceful dreaming brings.

A quiet hush
of gossamer
floats gently all around...

As downy snow
from angel wings
falls softly to the ground.
~ Torrey Miller

1 Use pattern or freehand sketch three feathers of approximately the same size on the right side of a sheet of vellum.

2 Using a stylus placed on top of a mouse pad, detail feathers by lightly pressing the stylus against the vellum and sketching softly.

3 Erase pencil marks; Freehand draw snowflake details using stylus pressed into the mouse pad.

Merry Christmas

Kristin's holiday mosaic only looks complicated. In reality, special scissors used for cutting stained-glass patterns make the process quick and easy. Using scissors, cut out a strip of paper, leaving a ¼" "leaded" space for a stained-glass look. Crop photos using a template (Frances Meyer). Position and layer photo shapes and die-cut letters on top of patterned paper (Autumn Leaves). Trace around shapes and letters with pencil. Draw design lines to use as a cutting guide. With a craft knife cut around shapes and letters ⅛" larger than actual photo for "leading." Starting at one corner of patterned paper, cut along guidelines with stained glass scissors, making sure to mount pieces on page as you go for easiest reassembly. Cut slices into photos and die-cut letters with scissors; mount.

Kristin Persson, Salem, Oregon

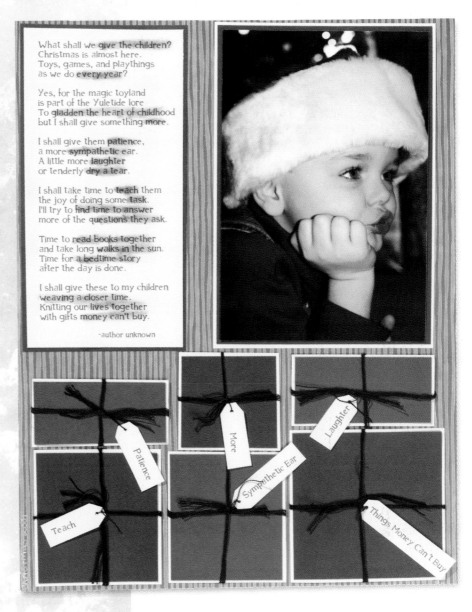

What shall we give the children?
Christmas is almost here.
Toys, games, and playthings
as we do every year?

Yes, for the magic toyland
is part of the Yuletide lore
To gladden the heart of childhood
but I shall give something more.

I shall give them patience,
a more sympathetic ear.
A little more laughter
or tenderly dry a tear.

I shall take time to teach them
the joy of doing some task.
I'll try to find time to answer
more of the questions they ask.

Time to read books together
and take long walks in the sun.
Time for a bedtime story
after the day is done.

I shall give these to my children
weaving a closer time.
Knitting our lives together
with gifts money can't buy.

-author unknown

What Shall We Give the Children?

Daintily wrapped presents tied with sentimental tags adorn Tina's heartwarming and meaningful page. Cut squares and rectangles in a variety of sizes from cranberry and green cardstock; mat on ivory cardstock. Tie with cotton threads (Making Memories). Print words for tags and poem on ivory cardstock. Freehand cut tag shapes around words; pierce a small hole at end and tie to "presents" with thread. Cut poem to size; highlight words with green chalk and mat. Double mat photo. Layer all pieces on patterned paper (Keeping Memories Alive).

Tina Chambers, Sardinia, Ohio

Trimming the Tree

Trudy adds sparkle and shine to a paper-torn background by adhering glittered embellishments. Tear strips of black cardstock; detail torn edges with black glitter before mounting on background. Using a craft knife and ruler, cut "windows" into torn background ¼" larger than photos; mat on purple cardstock. Mount photos in "windows" with self-adhesive foam spacers. Print partial title and journaling; cut to size and mat. Create glittered letters and embellishments by running gold and green cardstock through the adhesive application machine before coating with glitter. Cut title letters with template (Frances Meyer) and punch stars (EK Success, Emagination Crafts) from gold glittered cardstock. Mat letters on black cardstock; silhouette cut. Cut trees using template (Scrap Pagerz) from green glitter cardstock. Slice into sections; reassemble and mount on page. Decorate trees with bead strings (Magic Scraps). Wrap brown fibers (Magic Scraps) around small rectangle to create dimensional trunk.

Trudy Sigurdson,
Victoria, British Columbia, Canada

Merry Christmas

Liz's use of simple embellishments adds a warm and cozy feeling to her holiday page. Mat tan cardstock with red cardstock. Mat photos; mount. Cut title letters using template (Scrap Pagerz); outline with white gel pen. Mount on page with self-adhesive foam spacers. Print partial title, date and journaling. Cut title word to size; paper tear edges and mat. Cut month and date into circle shapes; mount on tags as shown. Cut jute; knot one end and slip on tag. Loop other end through title letter; slip on second tag and knot end. Cut journal block to size; paper tear edges and layer on matting detailed with jute bow. Mount pre-made embellishment at left side of journaling block.

Liz Ferrell, Clarksburg, Maryland

Christmas is near when the gingerbread men are made. Tiffany is just adding the icing & Smarties. December 2001

Gingerbread Men

Friendly, silhouette-cut and embossed gingerbread shapes make for a fanciful, festive border. Mat patterned paper (Sweetwater) with solid paper. Stamp gingerbread shapes (The Stamp Barn) onto brown paper with white ink; sprinkle with white embossing powder and set with heat embossing gun. Add colored details on shapes with pencil crayons (Sanford). Silhouette cut shapes; add green raffia bows. String metal stars (Provo Craft) onto green raffia strands across bottom of page. Mount gingerbread shapes over raffia with self-adhesive foam spacers. Mat photos; layer on page. Print title and journaling onto patterned paper (Provo Craft). Silhouette cut title letters; mat and silhouette cut again. Layer with self-adhesive foam spacers over green raffia. Mount one gingerbread shape and metal star with title.

Trudy Sigurdson, Victoria, British Columbia, Canada

Every Time a Bell Rings

Jodi gives her little angel a stunning pair of hand-crafted wings. Punch corners (Westrim) of background paper; mount over solid-colored paper. Craft feathers by following the instructions on the next page. Make wing shapes by layering feathers to form wings. Cut photo into oval shape; mat on gold paper trimmed with decorative scissors (Fiskars). Print journaling; cut to size and mat. Layer over sheer, gold-trimmed ribbon. Adhere sticker letters (Pioneer) on cream paper; silhouette cut and mount on sheer ribbon for title.

Jodi Amidei, Memory Makers

SONG-SATIONAL TITLES

Holiday songs are great for many things—including scrapbook page titles! Below, are some of the most popular holiday songs. Can you think of any scrapbook-worthy moments to illustrate them?

All I Want for Christmas Is My Two
    Front Teeth
Blue Christmas
Feliz Navidad
(There's No Place Like) Home for
    the Holidays
If Every Day was Like Christmas
White Christmas
It's Beginning to Look a Lot
    Like Christmas

Rockin' Around the Christmas Tree
Santa Baby
Feliz Navidad
Silent Night
The Twelve Days of Christmas
'Twas the Night Before Christmas
Up on the Housetop
We Wish You a Merry Christmas
Winter Wonderland
Deck the Halls

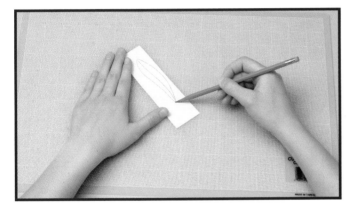

1 Create angel wings by freehand drawing different sized feathers on cream-colored cardstock. Or use the pattern found on page 93. Draw a straight line down the center of each feather.

2 Place feathers on a soft surface, such as a mouse pad. Using a wooden stylus, press firmly on the center line of the feathers, tracing from top to bottom to give the feather a curve.

3 Cut out feathers. Carefully cut into each feather, creating slanted, razor-thin slices. Stop cutting just before reaching the feather's center. Feather will begin to curl as you cut.

4 Turn feather over so penciled side is facing downward and lightly dust pigment powder over feather with a small brush to give gold tint.

Channnuka

Bold colors mixed with graphic lines and images work together to reflect Kelly's joyous holiday celebration. Mat medium blue cardstock over dark blue cardstock. Freehand cut small squares from lavender cardstock and wavy strips from dark blue cardstock; mount at bottom of page. Adhere stickers (Jewish Stickers) over squares. Cut large and small triangles from purple and yellow cardstocks; layer to create Star of David. Stamp swirl design (Hero Arts) with watermark ink onto yellow, dark blue and lavender cardstocks. Emboss with clear powder and set with heat embossing gun. Die cut hearts (Ellison) from embossed lavender and yellow cardstocks; mount on stars. Slice ¼" strips of yellow cardstock; mount diagonally. Cut title letters with template (Scrap Pagerz) from embossed dark blue paper; mount over strips at top of left page. Freehand cut large and small triangles for body and base of menorah. Slice ⅜" strips from yellow cardstock; cut candles in imperfect sizes. Freehand cut flames from purple and lavender cardstock. Mount glass beads (Magic Scraps) on small flames. Print journaling on blue cardstock; cut to size and mount on vellum. Mat photos on yellow and blue vellums.

Kelly Angard, Highlands Ranch, Colorado

Kwanzaa

Kwanzaa, a festival of thanksgiving celebrated by African-Americans each December, is observed through the lighting of candles and the exchange of gifts. Create Amy's colorful page with tribal-inspired border paper (Hot off The Press). Use a template (EK Success) to cut title letters from patterned paper (Hot off The Press); cut photo frame from same paper. Mount framed photo. Mat letters on black cardstock and mount across lower border. Add freehand cut candles, name and journaling blocks.

Amy Gustafson for Hot Off The Press

New Year's

Metallic patterned paper and embossed metal letters emphasize the excitement of a millennium celebration. Mat gold metallic cardstock with gray metallic cardstock. Double mat photos on metallic cardstocks. Print partial title, journaling and quote on vellum. Cut to size for title block; mat on metallic patterned cardstock (Club Scrap) and mount photo. Trim charm tops from metal letters and numbers (Making Memories). Press letters/numbers onto clear watermark pad; sprinkle with glittered embossing powder and set with heat embossing gun; mount on vellum with glue dots. Freehand cut large tag from vellum with quote; mat on metallic patterned cardstock. Attach silver eyelet and tie with fibers (Making Memories). Mount embossed metallic numbers. Add sunburst design to circle charm (Making Memories) with stencil (Club Scrap) and watermark pen (Tsukineko); emboss with gold and silver powder and set with embossing gun. Tie to tag with fibers.

Diana Hudson, Bakersfield, California

Jen and Alex

Jodi's words of love are perfectly expressed on a soft, romantic layout accented with elegant stamped and embossed details. Punch corner designs (All Night Media) on pink cardstock; mat with brown cardstock. Randomly stamp hearts with light pink ink. Wrap and mount sheer floral ribbon around white strip; layer over brown sheer ribbon as a vertical and horizontal border. Create stamped words by following the instructions on the right. Double mat large photo on left-hand page. Layer again on corner punched matting laced with twisted floral ribbon. Punch a ¼" hole at each corner of matting; feed ribbon strips through holes and mount in back. Mount matted photo with self-adhesive foam spacers over pink mulberry paper (PrintWorks). Handwrite title with marker; freehand cut into banner shape and mat. Punch small holes at top of banner and bottom of matting; link jewelry jump rings (Crafts, Etc.) together to form chain and "hang" banner. Secure banner with self-adhesive foam spacers. Mat photos for right-hand page; overlap and layer together on corner punched matting. "Hang" from horizontal border with jewelry jump rings. Write journaling on vellum; slip into vellum envelope made with template (JudiKins).

Jodi Amidei, Memory Makers

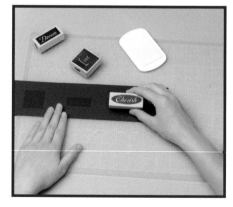

1 Stamp words (Stampa Rosa) onto brown cardstock with clear embossing ink.

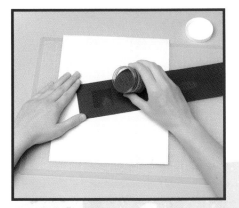

2 While ink is still wet, dust gold embossing powder over stamped images.

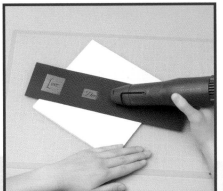

3 Using a heat gun, heat the embossing powder until it melts.

4 Cut out embossed word blocks and double mat. Lay over mulberry paper. Using a paint tip dipped lightly in water, draw around edges of mulberry and tear away. Mount torn shapes on border strips with self-adhesive foam spacers.

My Funny Valentine Brianna

Little love notes and a mini vellum pocket add perfect sentiment to Shauna's Valentine page. Mat color-tinted photos on white paper; layer with preprinted cut-out (Hot Off The Press (HOTP) over purple patterned paper (HOTP). Layer again over white paper trimmed with decorative scissors before mounting on patterned background paper (HOTP). Detail trimmed paper edges with black pen. Cut title letters with template (EK Success) from purple patterned paper. Layer over torn vellum strip with self-adhesive foam spacers. Mount small punched hearts to title letters; outline and detail with black pen. Print text for "love notes"; cut to size and mat. Create mini envelope with template (HOTP) from vellum. Mount heart die cut (HOTP) on envelope flap. Complete page with handwritten title words.

Shauna Berglund-Immel for Hot Off the Press

Beloved Child

A collection of soft and sweet embellishments detail Valerie's lovely tribute to her daughter. Diagonally tear embossed vellum (Paper Adventures); layer over light green cardstock. Double mat photo; tear edges of mulberry for second mat. Print poem on gray cardstock and title letters on pink cardstock. Cut poem to size and mat. Layer under photo corner on page. Cut 2" lace strips; mount at top of page with "stitched" buttons. Cut title letters; mount first letter on vellum tag (Making Memories) with lace strip. Mount balance of title letters on page. Cut three 2" squares from gray paper; mat on pink paper. Collage lace, mulberry paper (Paper Garden), button and punched hearts on matted squares.

Valerie Barton, Flowood, Mississippi

Valentine Love

Embellished creative lettering on handcrafted tags makes for an interesting title on Holle's romantic collage. Layer a wide strip of pink sparkled mesh (Magenta) over pink cardstock. Tear white paper and crumple; flatten and mount at top of page. Print journaling onto sparkled vellum (DMD); diagonally tear before matting on pink paper. Mount layers at upper right corner of layout. Freehand cut small tags from pink cardstock. Shape wire into "L"; layer over patterned mulberry paper (Pulsar Paper). Add gold heart nailhead (JewelCraft). Mount "O" letter pebble (Making Memories) over stamped words (Stampin' Up!); surround with red metal hearts (Scrapyard 329). Wrap top of tag with fibers (EK Success). Mount pre-printed die cut "V" (EK Success) on next tag under lavender mesh. Attach eyelet and tie fibers (EK Success). Write "E" on last tag with template (Wordsworth); color with pink marker. Mount heart sequins and wrap with tinsel (both, Magic Scraps). Mount embellished tags with self-adhesive foam spacers. Cut photo frame on left; tear all edges and curl gently with fingers. Cut frame for photo on right with craft knife; embellish with heart nailheads, metal hearts and tinsel. Add sheer ribbon bow; wrap around edges and secure.

Holle Wiktorek, Clarksville, Tennessee

SPRING

by Lois Duncan

This was a year when Spring forgot.

She stayed in the southlands far too long.

Ice lay slick on the garden path

And winter winds sang the robin's song.

The wood-burning fireplace lost its charm,

The beautiful snow turned slushy gray.

The mittens and jackets, the boots and scarves

Got damper and danker each passing day.

Then, full of apologies, Spring rushed home

To set things right. In a matter of hours

She changed all the icicles to leaves,

And all of the snowballs she turned to flowers.

Step Into My Garden

Gabrielle assembled a variety of creative techniques into an ensemble of garden-related novelties. Mat photo; brush edges of matting with brown chalk before mounting on background patterned paper (Provo Craft). Cut rectangles from cream-colored paper; brush around edges with brown chalk. Assemble laser die-cut gardening tools (Deluxe Cuts); mount. Stamp insects (Close To My Heart) on tags (Avery); detail with chalk. Stamp dragonfly image again on vellum; silhouette cut and chalk. Mount over previously stamped image; adhere at center of body, leaving wings free to lift off tag. Tie paper yarn (Making Memories) to tags. Punch flower shapes in three sizes from yellow paper. Layer graduated sizes; mount together with flower eyelet (Stamp Doctor). Mount flowerpot die cut (Making Memories) detailed with black chalk on rectangle with self-adhesive foam spacers. Cut paper yarn stems; mount with punched flower shapes coming out of pot. Print poem; cut to size and mount.

Gabrielle Mader, Whittier, California

Posing in the Poppies

Handcrafted flowers created from paper yarn, fibers and buttons are blooming along the bottom of Brooke's layout. Single and double mat photos; layer over brown cardstock. Print title and journaling. Silhouette cut title. Trim journaling to size and mat. Create "poppies" by following the instructions below. Tie small paper yarn (Making Memories) pieces onto fiber strips (On the Fringe) to look like leaves; stitch buttons with green fiber before mounting on page.

Brooke Smith, Anchorage, Alaska

1 Unravel strips of yellow and red paper yarn completely. Unravel green paper yarn only at the top to create flower stem.

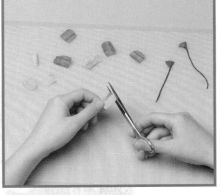

2 Trim red and yellow paper yarn into a U-shape to create flower petals.

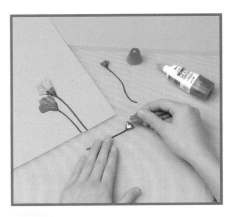

3 Assemble flowers on tan cardstock with adhesive. Arrange three petals into a fan shape, attach to stem, and then place the fourth petal vertically against the top of the stem.

Bloom, Emerge

Lynne presents the beauty of spring's sudden arrival on monochromatic, preprinted color-blocked paper. Mat two photos; layer with other photos on patterned paper (SEI). Print journaling onto vellum; cut to size before mounting on page with eyelets. Adhere title sticker letters (SEI). Handcraft tag from mauve paper; layer with paper-torn strip. Adhere pre-made flower embellishment (EK Success) and tuck hand-cut heart from textured paper behind torn strip.

Lynne Rigazio Mau, Channahon, Illinois

Joy, Dream, Love

Diana features blossoming flowers nestled in vellum layers for a soft, yet vibrantly colored layout. Mat yellow patterned paper (Close To My Heart) with brown cardstock. Mat two photos on yellow and brown cardstock. Slice a photo strip (Creative Imaginations) to use as an accent under vellum layer. Tear vellum pieces; layer with photos over background. Mount largest photo with yellow eyelets (Making Memories). Print title and journaling onto vellum. Tear around title words; gently roll torn edges with fingers. Distress journaling block; run vellum through adhesive machine for extra thickness. Tear around edges; crumple and flatten. Roll paper-torn edges with fingers before mounting. String beads (Magic Scraps) on copper-colored wire. Mount on title and journaling blocks with glue dots. Sprinkle seed beads on journaling block.

Diana Graham, Barrington, Illinois

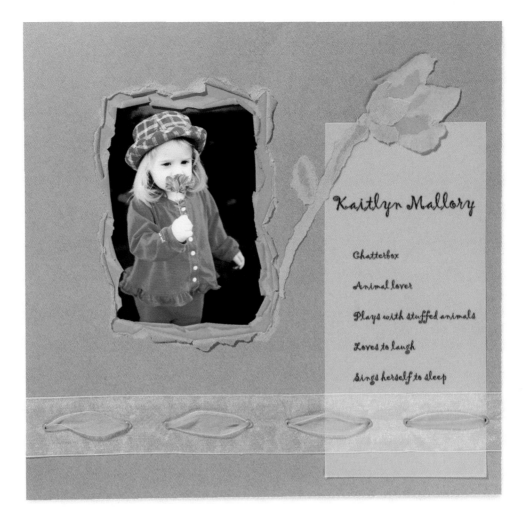

Kaitlyn Mallory

Chatterbox

Animal lover

Plays with stuffed animals

Loves to laugh

Sings herself to sleep

Kaitlyn Mallory

A paper-torn and curled frame provides a soft and interesting focal point on Valerie's elegant page. Lightly draw frame outline on pink cardstock. Punch through paper with scissors at center of frame and tear along penciled outline. Gently curl edges of torn paper with fingers. Repeat above steps with green cardstock, making a larger frame opening; mount over pink frame. Mount photo behind layered frame. Print journaling; cut to size and mount. Freehand draw flower shapes on green and pink cardstocks. Paper tear shapes; add yellow chalk details. Mount wide sheer ribbon across bottom of page; secure with pink eyelets. Weave thin sheer ribbon through eyelets.

Valerie Barton, Flowood, Mississippi

SPRING PHOTO CHECKLIST

- ❑ First communion
- ❑ Spring showers
- ❑ May flowers
- ❑ Gardening
- ❑ Opening day (baseball)
- ❑ Field day (track)
- ❑ Golf
- ❑ Soccer
- ❑ Easter
- ❑ Mother's Day
- ❑ Memorial Day
- ❑ Passover
- ❑ St. Patrick's Day
- ❑ Spring cleaning
- ❑ Prom
- ❑ Graduations
- ❑ Last day of school
- ❑ Spring break
- ❑ Mardi Gras
- ❑ Weddings
- ❑ Flying kites

Sunshine

Fanciful fibers are layered and stitched into whimsical designs that accent the title of Andrea's page. Triple mat photo on left-hand page. Mount three photos on one mat for right-hand page. Print title on green paper and journaling on vellum. Paper tear around title; layer over yellow paper with torn edges. Mount gold sun button (JHB International) on title strip. Paper tear around journaling on vellum; mount on page. Mount yellow-fringed fibers in a spiral design with glue; cut and mount small fiber pieces to complete sun. Lightly draw flower design on page with pencil. Pierce holes for stitching flower with needle or paper piercer. Stitch flower design with yellow and green embroidery threads (DMC).

Andrea Hautala, Olympia, Washington

Rain, Rain, Go Away

Jodi re-creates a raindrop-splattered window to reflect the blue mood of a child wanting to go outside and play. Stamp raindrops (All Night Media) onto vellum; sprinkle with clear embossing powder and set with heat embossing gun. Turn vellum over; layer stamped side over ¼" strips of white cardstock mounted vertically and horizontally to resemble windowpanes. Double and triple mat photos. Print title onto blue cardstock and journaling onto white cardstock. Cut journaling to size; mat with one photo onto vellum. Silhouette cut title letters; detail with craft knife. Layer triple matted photo onto textured, patterned paper (Club Scrap); mat again. Complete page with frosted glass pebbles randomly mounted with glue dots.

Jodi Amidei, Memory Makers

Grandma, How Does Your Garden Grow?

Sheila's colorfully stamped and silhouette cut vegetables dangle playfully among a variety of garden-themed embellishments. Layer large photo strip (Creative Imaginations) on left hand page over patterned background paper (Making Memories). Double and triple mat photos. Detail photo mats with paper-torn edges, flat eyelets and embroidery thread. Cut title letters (Sizzix) from solid-colored paper; mat and silhouette cut two times. Layer on page with self-adhesive foam spacers. Print balance of title and journaling onto solid-colored paper; cut to size and mat. Layer on page over metal mesh pieces. Stamp vegetables (Close To My Heart) with colored markers onto white paper. Create blended shades by using a variety of marker colors on back of stamp; lightly mist with water before stamping for a soft, washed look. Silhouette cut around shapes. Layer tomato and eggplant under paper-torn, metal mesh window frame on colored paper. Tie garden-themed charms (Charming Pages) with embroidery floss; tuck under paper-torn frame and mount. Dangle remaining vegetables from flat eyelets attached to photo mat with embroidery thread.

Sheila Boehmert, Island Lake, Illinois

Catch Me if You Can

Mary Anne's use of open space and simple embellishments makes for a visually appealing layout. Mat patterned paper (Provo Craft) onto solid ivory cardstock. Triple mat large photo; detail by dotting glitter glue on corners of second matting. Mat photos on solid-colored paper strips; mount along bottom of both pages. Print balance of title and journaling on vellum. Cut title letters using template (Scrap Pagerz) from solid green paper; mat on ivory cardstock and silhouette cut. Outline green letters with glitter glue before mounting on vellum. Cut photo corners from solid-colored paper; detail by dotting glitter glue on corners. Mount with vellum title/journaling block on page. Complete page with handcrafted bead dragonfly (pattern from *Beadlings* book by Klutz).

Mary Anne Walters, Monk Sherborne, Tadley, UK

Sunshine

Punched sun shapes not only reflect the warmth and joy of a little girl, but also the cheerful embroidered design on Sheila's daughter's hat. Layer strips of cardstock torn from patterned paper (Crafter's Workshop) over solid and patterned paper. Punch small (EK Success) and large (Emagination Crafts) sunbursts; layer over torn paper strips. Single and double mat photos on solid and patterned paper and vellum; tear a few edges. Adhere title letter stickers (Colorbök) to vellum; tear edges and mount on page with small gold brads.

Sheila Riddle, Elk River, Minnesota

Happiness Held Is the Seed

A charming succession of square-cut photos rests behind a printed vellum strip, giving just a hint of captured innocence in Martha's layout. Mat enlarged photos on solid paper; layer on patterned paper (Scrap Ease). Cut preprinted tags (EK Success); punch holes and tie with fibers (Making Memories) before mounting on page. Mount four 2" square photos next to each other at bottom of page. Print title quote onto vellum; cut to size and mount over photos with clear vellum tape (3M).

Martha Crowther, Salem, New Hampshire

The **W**ild vines twisted around the tree trunk and **I**t's branches. We were in awe of the beautiful Wi**S**teria as it dangled from above. One spring day I **T**alked the kids into posing for some very quick pictur**E**s along side the road to our subdivision. The imp**R**omptu photo shoot ended abruptly once the buzzing bees attacked their heads! But capturing **A** perfect spring photo was worth the effort.

Wisteria

Hanging wisteria vines created from punched and paper-torn shapes drape elegantly across the top of Valerie's page. Mat photos on lavender cardstock with paper-torn edges; detail with purple chalk around edges. Print journaling on lavender cardstock; cut to size and mat. Shade title letters with purple chalk. Attach purple eyelets under journaling; loop beaded and twisted wire embellishment through eyelets. Create wisteria vines by tearing and folding strips of brown mulberry paper into vine shapes; mount along top of page. Freehand draw leaf shapes onto green cardstock; paper tear along lines, crumple and shade with green chalk. Layer on vines. Create wisteria flower clusters by following the instructions to the left and below.

Valerie Barton, Flowood, Mississippi

1 Punch out 12-14 small (1") circles for each Wisteria bunch you plan to create.

2 Fold left edge of punched circle toward center. Overlap by folding right edge of circle inward to form petal.

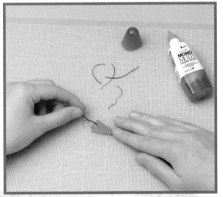

3 Cut paper whispers. The thinner they are, the more they will curl. Glue paper whispers on the inside of folded punched shapes, allowing a small strip to project beyond the "petals".

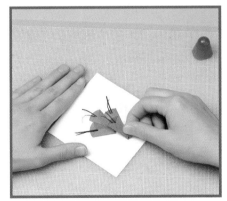

4 Layer flowers on the page, arranging until you achieve the desired effect.

Easter 2002

A colorfully detailed stained-glass design frames a photo of Heidi's daughters in their holiday best. Cut vellum into quadrants; attach eyelets and link pieces with pink ribbon woven through the eyelets. Layer over patterned background paper (Making Memories). Print title on vellum. Trace over letters with embossing pen; sprinkle with embossing powder and set with heat gun. Add color to spaces in letters with pink marker; silhouette cut and mount on page. Create "stained glass" design on 8½ x 6½" piece of vellum paper. Place photo at center; trace around as guide; remove photo. Draw design lines with pencil; color in with markers. Mount strips and pieces of paper yarn (Making Memories) as "leaded lines" over penciled guidelines with glue. Layer entire design over white paper. Mount photo at center of design.

Heidi Schueller, Waukesha, Wisconsin

Happy Easter

Valerie's holiday photos and religious symbols are "hung" from a die-cut title border adorned with buttons and crystal lacquered leaves. Layer solid and patterned (Paper Fever) papers torn along the bottom edge over light yellow cardstock. Die cut letters (Accu-Cut) into vellum; set die-cut letters aside and use die-cut negative space. Tear bottom edge of vellum and mount with gold brads. Double mat photos with solid and patterned papers. Paper tear edges of one mat. Cut cross into vellum with craft knife before mounting over photo. Cut freehand drawn cross from solid tan paper. Draw decorative lines with brown marker. Trace over marker lines with crystal lacquer for dimension. Freehand cut leaves from solid green paper; detail with crystal lacquer (Sakura Hobby Craft). Mount leaves inside of title letters and on cross with self-adhesive foam spacers. Attach eyelets to cross and photos. Stitch buttons with jute string; loop ends through eyelets and tie. Mount buttons with self-adhesive foam spacers along border. Attach leaves behind buttons.

Valerie Barton, Flowood, Mississippi

Passover

Kelly tells the powerful story of Passover with colorful text and Judaic stickers adhered on a border and handcrafted tags. Create border with large stickers (Jewish Stickers) adhered to solid paper; mount on matted cardstock strip. Cut title with template (Scrap Pagerz); outline with fine-tip black pen. Mount matted sticker strip and letters on patterned paper (Scrappin' Dreams) with self-adhesive foam spacers; layer on purple background paper (Karen Foster Design). Adhere balance of title letter stickers (Making Memories). Print journaling onto vellum. Cut to size; frame with thin strips of black cardstock. Layer over colorful fiber scraps glued to white cardstock strip for a hint of decorative color. Mat photos; mount on page. Adhere small stickers to white matted strip. Layer over freehand cut matted tags tied with fibers (Making Memories).

Kelly Angard, Highlands Ranch, Colorado

Madeleine

Mary Anne's whimsically embellished tags provide a colorful contrast to a subtle, muted background. Cut title letters using template (Scrap Pagerz) from patterned paper (Paper Adventures). Mat on purple cardstock; silhouette cut. Layer letters on border strip matted with torn blue mulberry paper. Layer again on wide patterned paper strip with torn mulberry border. Adhere vellum flower stickers (Stickopotamus) to border strip with self-adhesive foam spacers. Single and triple mat photos; tear edges of mulberry matting. Press small thin metal washers onto clear embossing pad; sprinkle with blue embossing powder and set with heat gun. Embellish tags with vellum flower stickers, embossed washers, fibers (Memory Crafts) and letter stickers (Colorbök). Print journaling onto teal cardstock; cut to size and tear bottom edge. Mount on page under thin patterned paper slice. Mount vellum flowers with self-adhesive foam spacers.

Mary Anne Walters, Monk Sherborne, Tadley, UK

Haley, Age 5

Lisa's vibrant, rainbow-colored tags tied with chunky braided fibers provide the perfect place for journaling details. Mount enlarged and cropped photo on solid-colored cardstock. Shade tags (DMD) with complementary chalk colors, blending well with fingers. Write journaling on tags with black fine-tip pen. Braid fibers (DMC) on tags before mounting over ribbon with self-adhesive foam spacers.

Lisa Francis, New Castle, Indiana

A Mother's Love

Softly torn and curled paper edges add a sweet, elegant look to Brandi's sentimental page. Tear yellow paper strip for border; mount at left side of page over blue cardstock. Gently curl edges with fingers. Tear matting for photos from yellow paper; tear piece from side of matting for a soft, unique detail. Pierce holes and lace with embroidery thread. Mount photos and buttons on torn matting. Stamp butterfly shapes (Hero Arts) with light blue ink on ivory paper; silhouette cut and mount with self-adhesive foam spacers. Print title words on ivory cardstock. Tear and chalk around edges using a metal-edged ruler as a guide.

Brandi Ginn, Lafayette, Colorado

Mommy and Megan 1986

Peggy captures the serenity of a read-aloud moment shared with her daughter on Mother's Day 1986 in this simple but striking page. Offset photo on light blue mat. Mat again over vellum and then hand torn light brown cardstock before attaching to page. Print journaling block on vellum; tear. Punch holes in lower edge of journaling block; thread with white fiber; mount. Wrap fiber horizontally around upper page and journaling block. Punch sun shapes from brown cardstock and vellum; layer and adhere to page over fiber. Tear title block. Hand stitch stems and leaves and attach to flower eyelets. Punch small holes on background and thread flowers and stems through holes to secure; tie knots on backside of paper. Lay torn paper title over "stem" bottoms.

Peggy Roarty, Council Bluffs, Iowa

Beauty in Bloom

Gayla highlights the beauty of her daughters among the blue bonnets with enlarged photo border strips. Slice enlarged photos for borders; mount over blue background cardstock leaving ½" border. Mat photos; layer over green patterned paper (Club Scrap). Print title and journaling onto vellum; mount with eyelets over photo pieces sliced into strips and cut into squares.

Gayla Feachen, Irving, Texas

Fancy Little Violets

Heidi stamped an imaginative floral background onto textured paper to create a uniquely blooming background. Create the background by following the instructions below. Double mat photos. Adhere purple title letter stickers (Sandylion) on yellow paper; tear edges. Adhere white title letter stickers (Creative Memories) to vellum squares; mount on page. Punch flowers (EK Success) and mini circles from purple and yellow paper; mount along title and at bottom of page with flower eyelets (Making Memories).

Heidi Schueller, Waukesha, Wisconsin

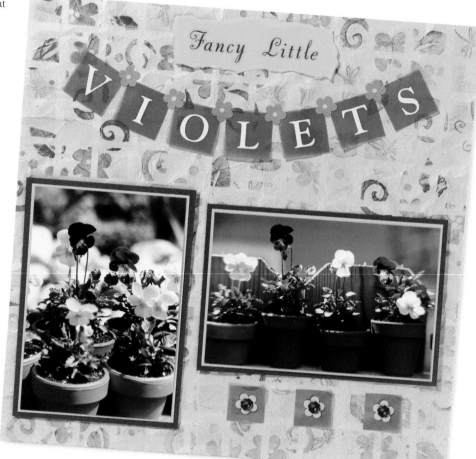

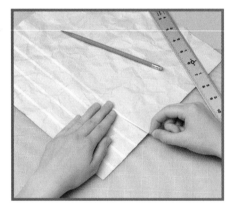

1 Crumple paper and then flatten. Using a ruler, make a tick mark at 1" intervals across the bottom of the paper. When finished, mark left and right sides of the paper in a similar manner, forming a grid.

2 Ink floral stamp pad with two different ink colors. Blot by stamping once on scrap paper.

3 Stamp image over masked squares. To avoid an overpowering image, stamp cardstock three or four times before re-inking.

4 Lightly dust stamped cardstock with chalk. Gently wipe one time with fingers or cotton ball. Remove masking tape to reveal stamped image. Erase tick marks and finish layout.

Happy Last Day of School

A variety of type fonts arranged on layers of complementary-colored papers provides visual interest to Oksanna's layout. Layer green patterned paper (Carolee's Creations) over yellow cardstock. Silhouette cut preprinted title (Carolee's Creations); mount with patterned paper frame (Carolee's Creations) over background with photo at center. Print partial title on yellow cardstock; cut to size and trim with decorative scissors (Fiskars). Detail curved edges with dimensional fabric paint (Duncan); double mat. Write partial title with marker on yellow paper scrap; double mat. Die cut letters (EZ2Cut) for balance of title from blue cardstock; outline with black fine-tip pen. Punch daisies (Fiskars) from yellow cardstock; mount gems at centers before layering on title letters.

Oksanna Pope, Los Gatos, California

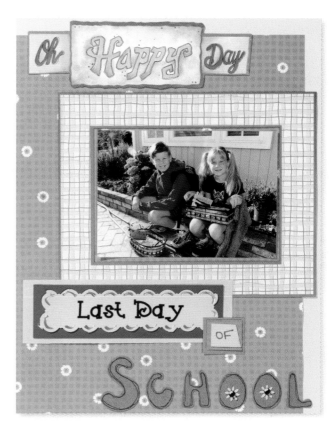

Golf

The sophisticated essence of the timeless game of golf is featured on Kelli's three-dimensional embellishment-filled page. Mat photos on solid-colored cardstock and torn mulberry paper (Paper Adventures); mount on solid-colored background. Punch diamond shapes from navy blue cardstock; mount end-to-end on silver metallic cardstock; silhouette cut. Mount with self-adhesive foam spacers on torn mulberry photo mat. Adhere premade golf club stickers (EK Success) on navy blue cardstock. Detail with black chalk around edges; mat on torn mulberry paper. Punch title letters (EK Success) from navy blue cardstock; mat on silver metallic cardstock and silhouette cut. Layer letters on torn pieces of mulberry paper; mount on page with self-adhesive foam spacers. Adhere golf bag and golf ball stickers at bottom of page under torn mulberry paper strip. Complete page with journaling.

Kelli Noto, Centennial, Colorado

Kindergarten Graduation

Kelli's visually dramatic presentation of her son's graduation portrait is bordered with striking stamped and embossed letters. Stamp large title letters with gold ink along side of page. Write balance of title along top of page with gold embossing pen. Mount strips of heavy double-sided tape (Suze Weinberg) around title words. Sprinkle written words, stamped letters and double-sided tape with gold ultra thick embossing enamel (RANGER, Suze Weinberg); set with heat embossing gun. Single and double mat photos on gold metallic cardstock and vellum. Print journaling onto metallic vellum; mat and mount on page with self-adhesive foam spacers. Adhere strips of heavy double-sided tape on metallic vellum rectangle; sprinkle with black embossing enamel. Set with heat embossing gun. Mount graduation cap and gown (EK Success) on metallic vellum.

Kelli Noto, Centennial, Colorado

SUMMER

by Lois Duncan

The wealth of summer
Is dreamer's gold.
For so short a time
It is ours to hold—
Gold in the meadow,
Gold by the stream,
Riches enough for
a miser's dream.

Golden currency,
Ours to spend,
And here, where the sun
Warmed grasses bend,
A golden mattress
On which to lie
As the sun sinks low
In a golden sky.

Red – Caroline
Orange – Matthew
Yellow – Oliver
Green – Jameel
Blue – Robby
Purple – Hugh W.

Rainbow popsicles taste so sweet
They are the only things we want to eat.
In the hot, hot sun they cool our tongue
We eat them each day until summer is done.
They drip on the ground melted by the sun
Blending into a sticky mess, fun, fun, fun.

June 2002

Rainbow Popsicles

Shannon's cleverly wrapped "popsicles" make for a vibrant and colorful addition along the bottom of her layout. Slice ½" strips of cardstock in six colors; mount ⅛" apart. Print journaling and names onto white cardstock; cut to size. Mat photos and journaling six times on colored cardstocks. Cut title letters from template (EK Success) in a variety of colors; outline with black fine-tip pen. Cut names to size; mat on colored cardstocks. Make "popsicles" by slicing 1¼" strips of colored cardstock, rounding edges at one end. Wrap slices with crumpled page protectors to resemble popsicle packaging; mount plastic at back of strip, then layer on bottom of page .

Shannon Taylor, Bristol, Tennessee

Warning! Not for Adult Use

Sandra's graphic, bold layout tells the humorous story of a slip-and-slide adventure gone wrong. Print title and journaling on yellow cardstock. Slice ⅜" and ¾" strips of red cardstock; mount at top and bottom of page. Cut a 7¾ x 12" piece of red cardstock; mount below title. Mount photos on yellow cardstock; tear bottom edge of matting. Mount red buttons on torn matting.

Sandra Stephens, Eden Prairie, Minnesota

Summertime Nicole

Linda captures the sweet essence of innocent childhood moments with handmade and detailed daisies scattered among sepia-toned snapshots. Tear edges of tan cardstock; shade with brown chalk before mounting on patterned background paper (Debbie Mumm). Double mat photos; layer on page. Cut title letters with template (Cut-It-Up) from two shades of blue cardstock. Shade letters with blue chalk for dimension before mounting on blue paper-torn strip. Freehand draw daisies on yellow cardstock; silhouette cut. Outline flower petals with yellow marker; shade center of flower and inner part of petals with brown chalk. Add pen details. Cut center of flower from brown cardstock; add texture with cut pieces of embroidery threads glued to center of flower. Mount flowers on page. Print journaling on brown cardstock; tear edges and shade with brown chalk. Mount flower charm tied with embroidery thread under name.

Linda Cummings, Murfreesboro, Tennessee
Photos, Regina Robinson, Lebanon, Tennessee

The Swing

Diana's desire to design a charming page with an old-fashioned look is achieved by using paper and embellishments that complement the sepia-toned photos. Double mat patterned background paper (Karen Foster Design) with patterned paper (Creative Imaginations) mounted on solid paper with eyelets. Print large photo with title; mount on page; detail at corners with fiber stitches (EK Success). Use square punch for small photo images. Distress edges of tags (Avery) with scissors and detail with brown colored pencil for antiqued look. Mount photos and buttons on tags. Tie with fibers; dangle from eyelets attached to matted photo. Print poem on tag; add chalk detail and distress edges for antiqued look. Mount wooden buttons and tie with fiber before mounting on page.

Diana Graham, Barrington, Illinois

Fishing Dad

Jodi hand-tied flies to lend an authentic feel to her page, which reflects her father's love for fly fishing. Stamp and clear emboss background landscape design with a variety of stamped designs (PSX Design, Coronado Island Stamping, Stampscapes). Slice two strips of solid-colored paper; attach small brads. Mount net on left side of layout, wrapping around and securing to back of page with glue dots. Mount hand-tied flies to ovals cut using a template or oval cutter. Cut oval frames; mat and mount with foam tape for a dimensional effect. Stamp and emboss fish (PSX Design) and title letters (Plaid); silhouette cut. Punch small holes at mouth of fish; attach wire through holes. Triple mat photo. Dangle wired fish from small brads mounted on third photo mat; secure fish with self-adhesive foam spacers. Print journaling onto vellum. Cut to size and mount on page with small brads.

Jodi Amidei, Memory Makers

Nature Girl

Torrey crafted a window of opportunity for dangling title letters and punched shapes. Create background with various stamped and embossed nature images (All Night Media, Stampin' Up!, Hero Arts). Cut window into background paper; mount patterned paper (EK Success) behind window with foam tape to create a raised effect. Attach three metal title letters (Making Memories) to vellum tags (Making Memories); layer with punched leaf shapes (Emagination Crafts, Punch Bunch) detailed with chalk. Attach colored eyelets to balance of metal letters. "Hang" letters and tags with fiber (On The Surface) by securing with either glue dots or other strong adhesive. Cut matted frame larger than window with craft knife; mount over background paper. Print partial title and journaling; tear around edges. Detail with chalk and curl paper edges inward with fingers. Attach eyelets; dangle title word with fiber from window frame. Mount journaling block on page. Triple mat photo; mount.

Torrey Miller, Thornton, Colorado

Lazy Summer Days

Serendipity squares, crafted from collaged strips of patterned paper, make for a visually interesting border. Tear two 1" strips of gold metallic cardstock; mount at top and bottom of page. Layer patterned paper (Keeping Memories Alive, Hot Off the Press, Paper Adventures) strips on a large piece of teal cardstock. Punch 1½" squares from collaged cardstock. Embellish squares with gold embroidery thread, sea-life charms and micro glass beads. Slice a 1⅛" strip from enlarged photo; cut strip into squares. Mount all photo pieces on tan cardstock. Double mat smaller photos together. Print title and journaling onto blue and tan cardstock. Silhouette cut large title word; cut smaller words to size and mat. Cut journaling block to size; slice a serendipity square into thirds and mount at top of journaling block. Assemble shaker box by cutting one 7⅝ x 2⅜" rectangle from patterned paper and one 7⅝ x 2⅜" rectangle from teal cardstock. Slice a 6¾ x 1¾" window into rectangle with craft knife. Cut a piece of clear, plastic sheet in the same size; mount behind window. Cut strips of self-adhesive foam spacer tape; mount along back of window frame. Add broken seashells and micro glass beads; seal with last strip of foam tape. Mount silhouette cut title word and squares on top of shaker box.

Antuanette Wheeler, Center Hill, Florida

Endless Beauty

Brooke's shaker box holds tiny treasures from the sea, highlighting realistic details from photos. Tear two shades of tan cardstock; chalk. Mount the lighter cardstock at the bottom of a blue cardstock background. Slice curved triangle into corners of darker tan cardstock with a craft knife. Cut page protector, or other plastic sheet, large enough to cover window; mount at back of cardstock window. Cut strips of self-adhesive foam tape; adhere behind two sides of the window. Fill with small shells; seal with another piece of foam tape. Double mat photos; paper tear edges of second matting before mounting on page. Print title and journaling on tan cardstock. Silhouette cut title; mount at top of page. Cut journaling to size; mount on photo. Mount metallic fibers (On the Fringe) on second matting of large photo. Randomly glue small seed beads on title, matting and torn strips.

Brooke Smith, Anchorage, Alaska

Sweet Taste

Heidi's creative collection of colored glass pebbles and title fonts is assembled on a delightful layout that celebrates summer. Slice a 2½" strip of magenta cardstock at top of page; mount on dark blue background cardstock. Cut five 1¾" squares from white cardstock; mat on yellow cardstock and mount on border strip. Arrange colored glass and word pebbles (The Beadery) on squares. Mount with a strong adhesive. Outline squares with fuzzy fibers (Magic Scraps). Mat photos; outline smaller photos with fuzzy fibers. Print title on a variety of colored cardstocks. Cut words to size; piece together to form one large text block. Print journaling on purple cardstock, leaving room for embellishment at top. Cut to size; attach purple flower eyelets. String letter beads on fiber; mount through eyelets and secure at back of cardstock before mounting on page.

Heidi Schueller, Waukesha, Wisconsin

The View From the Porch

Pam memorializes favorite moments spent rocking on her front porch with conversational journaling and a refreshing glass of lemonade. Triple mat yellow patterned paper (Doodlebug Design) for background. Mount photos on matted background. Print title and journaling on vellum; cut oval into vellum before mounting on page. Assemble laser die cut glass of lemonade (Deluxe Cuts); mount over vellum.

Pam Easley, Bentonia, Mississippi

Each New Wave

A succession of small snapshots creates a slide show effect highlighting a fun day of frolicking on the beach. Crop photos to 1½ x 2"; mount in a vertical row on patterned paper (EK Success). Mat large photo on blue patterned paper (Two Busy Moms). Print journaling on vellum; paper tear around edges and layer at bottom of page. Cut pre-printed tag (EK Success); tie with fibers (Making Memories) before mounting on page. Mount smallest photo under plastic slide (Pakon).

Martha Crowther, Salem, New Hampshire

Each new wave rearranges the patterns in the sand so we may pretend that our footsteps are the first.

August · 2002 · Having Fun · Hampton Beach · WAVES · Sunshine · cold water

Down By the Sea

Photo die cuts, twine and netting bring images of the ocean to life on Martha's textured title block. Tear two strips of yellow cardstock; mount horizontally over light blue cardstock. Layer twine, title and photo die cuts (Ivy Cottage, Paper House Productions) over torn paper strips. Mount plastic netting over layers with glue dots. Mat two enlarged photos together on yellow cardstock; mount on page. Journal.

Martha Crowther, Salem, New Hampshire

Sandcastles

Martha's choice of imaged paper, torn and layered underneath an enlarged photo conjures images of soft sand between your toes. Diagonally tear photo paper; layer over solid background paper. Mat enlarged photo on yellow cardstock; mount inset photo at upper left corner with self-adhesive foam spacers. Attach fibers (Making Memories) around edges of matting with glue dots. Crop smaller photos; layer on page. Tie fibers to metal clips; attach to photos. Punch hole at top left corner of die cut (Ivy Cottage); tie fibers and mount on page.

Martha Crowther, Salem, New Hampshire

SUMMER PHOTO CHECKLIST

- ❑ Opening the pool
- ❑ Last day of school
- ❑ First day of camp
- ❑ Garage sales
- ❑ Camping trips
- ❑ Family reunions
- ❑ Road trips
- ❑ Barbecues
- ❑ Outdoor festivals and concerts
- ❑ Fourth of July
- ❑ Father's Day
- ❑ Amusement parks
- ❑ Lemonade stands
- ❑ Water sports (skiing, swimming, sunbathing, etc)
- ❑ Vacations (beach or otherwise)
- ❑ Home improvements
- ❑ Lawn mowing
- ❑ Taking care of a new puppy or kitten
- ❑ Summer jobs
- ❑ Summer school
- ❑ Baseball games

Mr. Sandman

A soft, textured background accented with eclectic details complements Martha's enlarged photo of her son romping in the sand. Texture green background by gently crumpling cardstock; flatten. Mat enlarged photo on light blue cardstock; mount on page. Print title on vellum; tear to size and mount. Cut preprinted tags (EK Success) to size; punch holes at top and tie fibers (Making Memories). Complete page with a collection of mounted fibers, sea glass and shells at lower right-hand photo corner.

Martha Crowther, Salem, New Hampshire

The Patriotic Creed

Martha's soft paper-torn background is a nice contrast to the sharp, striking lines of the American flag. Tear strips of navy blue, tan and red cardstocks; collage and layer over red cardstock background. Mat enlarged photo on navy blue cardstock. Double mat smaller photo; paper tear edges of second mat. Print poem on tan cardstock; tear edges. Mat on navy cardstock; paper tear edges before mounting on page. Mount pre-made patriotic tag (EK Success) to complete page.

Martha Crowther, Salem, New Hampshire

Free to Be Just Anna

Pam builds on the theme of freedom by capturing her daughter's unabashed antics on patriotic paper. Tear edges of 12 x 12" vellum for both pages; layer over patterned paper (K & Company.) Double mat large photo on solid and patterned paper; attach star eyelets (Happy Hammer) around second matting. Mount photos on right hand page. Print title, journaling and descriptive words on vellum. Tear all to size; mount title words to page with small brads. Mount descriptive words on photos and journaling with clear vellum tape. String letter (Darice) and metallic beads on copper wire; curl edges into swirls to hold beads in place; mount on page with glue dots.

Pam Easley, Bentonia, Mississippi

The Summer That Kevin Didn't Play Ball

Kelli's sharp attention to detail turns ordinary strips of cardstock into nostalgic artwork. To create "antiqued" paper baseball border see the instructions below. Print title and journaling on "antiqued" paper. Slice strip from title block; pierce holes and lace like border. Cut dialogue journaling to size; mat on black cardstock. Mat photos on black and "antiqued" cardstock; mount.

Kelli Noto, Centennial, Colorado

THE SUMMER THAT KEVIN DIDN'T PLAY BALL.

One day in the summer of 2002, seemingly out of the blue, Kevin said, "Mom, I don't want to play baseball this summer."

"Really?" I asked.

I had taken for granted that my boys would always play baseball on sultry, summer evenings. "Tell me why, sweetie."

"It's boring, Mom. I'm the littlest kid on the team, so the coach always puts me in left field." There was a sadness is his eyes. "Mom, the ball never goes to left field."

"I see, honey," I said. "What about batting? Do you enjoy the batting?"

I was careful not to let Kevin see my own disappointment. I didn't want the fact that I enjoyed watching him play influence a decision that needed to be his alone.

"Well," Kevin said, "I only bat once and then I wait for all the other kids on both teams to take their turns. That's an awful lot of waiting, Mom."

"I see," I said. And I did see. "Is there something else that you'd like to sign up for?"

"How about tennis!" Kevin asked.

Tennis sounded perfect for a little boy who was relegated to left field and wanted a few more turns at whacking a ball.

And that is why, in the summer he was seven, Kevin didn't play baseball.

1 Lightly spray a cream-colored paper strip with water and crumple. Gently flatten.

2 Iron crumpled paper strip with steam iron. Brush lightly with brown chalk to add definition. Edges should tear slightly or soften as you flatten out the strip.

3 Fold ¼" of the paper strip under and punch holes every ½" along this folded edge with a paper piercing tool or needle.

Challengers Baseball

Janice photojournals a delightful activity enjoyed by her special-needs son over the summer. Double mat three photos on white cardstock; mount at top of left page and bottom of right page. Single mat other photos. Print journaling on tan paper; cut to size. Detail edges with brown chalk and black fine-tip pen. Layer over preprinted die-cut baseball (EK Success). Print title; silhouette cut and mount on left page. Mount die-cut baseball hat (EK Success) under title.

Janice Carson, Hamilton, Ontario, Canada

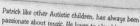

Patrick like other Autistic children, has always been passionate about music. He loves to play his keyboard, drum machine and listen to his Abba CD.

Patrick's Special Needs Worker, Heather suggested that we introduce him to the "Challengers Baseball League". At first we were a little hesitant because he has never shown an interest in sports and he gets quite agitated when he is bored. Heather took him out the first night to see how Patrick would react. Surprisingly, he had a wonderful time. It is so nice to see Patrick enjoy an activity.

From that point on, Patrick played "baseball" every Tuesday night for the entire summer.

He made many improvements during the season. He gained a stronger throwing arm and was very eager to hit the ball off the tee. We are thrilled with Patrick's accomplishments this baseball season!

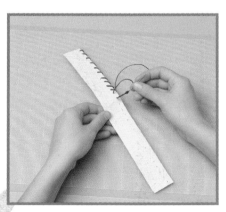

4 Using an over-under "lacing stitch," weave down entire folded strip with red thread to emulate baseball stitching. Create right and left-sided borders. Mount together down the left side of page.

Special Daddy Moments

Oksanna captures a treasured moment between father and daughter with torn vellum and punched embellishments. Double mat photo on burgundy vellum and green handmade (DMD) paper. Dot matting edges with gold dimensional fabric paint (Duncan). Mount on patterned background paper (Design Originals). Print title and journaling on vellum. Cut journaling to size; mat on tan cardstock before layering over green paper and burgundy vellum rectangles. Punch fern leaves (Punch Bunch) from light green cardstock; mount around upper left edges of matted journaling. Cut large title letter using template (C-Thru Ruler) from vellum; outline with black fine-tip pen. Layer large letter, title block and tan cardstock square and mount on page. Tear vellum pieces in graduated circle shapes; stamp swirl design (All Night Media) on smallest piece. Mount layered pieces together with small gold brad. Layer at corners with punched fern leaves.

Oksanna Pope, Los Gatos, California

Father's Day

Title letters imprinted in thick copper embossing enamel (Ranger) make for an impressive masculine title. Cut circles from two-sided thick tape (Suze Weinberg); sprinkle with copper ultra thick embossing enamel (Ranger). Set with heat embossing gun; Repeat 2-3 times. When last layer is still warm, press letter stamps (Hero Arts) into enamel. Mat photos on tan cardstock. Cut frame for large photo from light green cardstock; slice window slightly larger than matted photo. Mount with self-adhesive foam tape. Freehand cut tag; mat and silhouette cut. Emboss self-adhesive foam spacer letters and edges of tag with copper embossing enamel. Cut square from green cardstock for embellished journaling. Tie fibers (On The Surface) to copper tag (Anima Designs); mount fishing fly to tag. Stamp letters (Hero Arts) on small piece of wood veneer; mat on green cardstock. Cut patterned paper (Paper Garden) to fit behind copper bookplate (Anima Designs); mount tile letters (Hasbro) in bookplate window.

Kelli Noto, Centennial, Colorado

Summer Barbecue

Dana knows summer just wouldn't be the same without family barbecues, watermelon and...ants! Double mat photos on patterned (Frances Meyer) and solid papers; layer on page. Freehand draw ant and line border with red and black fine-tip pens. Print title words on red cardstock and journaling on white cardstock. Freehand cut red cardstock with title words into watermelon slice shapes; double mat on white and green cardstocks. Draw seed details with fine-tip black pen. Freehand craft small watermelon slices in same manner; mount on photos with journaling. Cut journaling block to size and mat; adhere ant stickers (Mrs. Grossman's).

Dana Forti, Claremont, California

BBQ

Original paper-pieced and shaker box food and condiments add a touch of whimsy to Karen's BBQ table. Slice two 2½" strips of patterned paper (Scrapbook Sally); mount along page bottom as tablecloth. Enlarge patterns, found on page 93, for paper-pieced food and condiments. Trace patterns onto appropriate colors of cardstock, cut out and layer into designs. Add chalk and pen line details to finished pieces. To create salt and pepper shakers and watermelon follow the directions below. Print journaling; cut to size. Mat photos and journaling on red cardstock. Die cut shadow title letters (Sizzix) from red and black cardstocks; layer and mount. Punch small ant (EK Success); mount.

Karen Cobb, Victoria, British Columbia, Canada

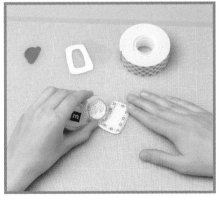

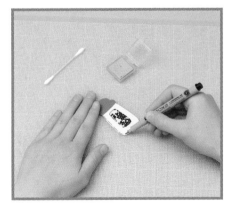

1 Double cut pattern pieces (page 93) for salt/pepper shakers and watermelon. Slice windows into one set of salt/pepper shakers and watermelon with craft knife. Leave second set uncut. From a plastic sheet or page protector cut one pattern of each piece.

2 Mount cut plastic sheet or page protector to back of window. Cut self-adhesive foam tape; adhere to all sides.

3 Fill salt and pepper shakers with white and black seed beads. Fill watermelon with punched teardrop shapes. Seal shaker boxes by placing back piece on top of foam adhesive. Turn over and attach to page.

Some Things Money Can't Buy...

Alison highlights the "treasures" in her life with a clean and simple layout adorned with realistic coin photo stickers. Mat brown cardstock with black cardstock. Tear two strips of vellum, one wider than the other; mount on page. Print title/journaling on white cardstock; cut to size. Mat journaling and enlarged photo on tan cardstock before layering over wide torn vellum strip. Adhere coin stickers (Creative Imaginations) on matted journaling block. Crop smaller photos into 2⅛" squares; mat on tan cardstock and mount over thin, torn vellum strip.

Alison Beachem, San Diego, California

Scootin'

A combination of silver metallic fiber, paper, eyelets and brads reflects Dee's son's love for the "cool" sport of scootin'. Horizontally tear patterned bottom edge of vellum (Colorbök); mount with small silver brads. Attach silver eyelets to bottom of photos. Cut 5" pieces of metallic fibers (On the Fringe); loop through eyelets and adhere to backs of photos. Mount photos over patterned vellum. Print journaling on vellum; cut to size and mount with small black brads. Craft serendipity squares with collaged layers of glossy black cardstock, mulberry paper, vellum, glitter and diamond glaze (JudiKins). Cut or punch seven 1½" squares from completed serendipity design; Mount. Cut title letters with template (Provo Craft) from silver metallic cardstock. Attach large silver eyelets to center of "O" letters. Attach small silver eyelets at top of each letter. Loop loose fiber ends through eyelets; adhere on backs of letters. Mount letters atop serendipity squares.

Dee Gallimore-Perry, Griswold, Connecticut

Hearts Rock

Mary Anne features a special family tradition with dimensionally accented photos alongside theme-appropriate die cuts. Slice two 3½" wide strips of red cardstock and two ½" wide strips of brown cardstock. Layer on page as top and bottom borders. Print titles on ivory and black cardstocks; print journaling on white cardstock. Silhouette cut title word on ivory cardstock. Cut title letters on black cardstock into retro-looking squares. Mount pre-printed die-cut images (EK Success) on border strips. Using a craft knife, slice out photo detail to be highlighted. Mat on cardstock and silhouette cut; remount on photo, covering area that was cut. Mat photo on red cardstock. Triple mat large photo; tear mulberry paper (Paper Adventures) on third matting. Mount rock to page with wire.

Mary Anne Walters, Monk Sherborne, Tadley, UK

When Jackson was 3 years old, we took him to Brighton to see a train show. While walking on the beach he reached down and picked up a rock when he gave it to me, I could see it was in the shape of a heart. Jack said "Just because I love you, Mom." Then and there began a tradition that has lasted for the last 6 years. Everywhere we go walking, when there are rocks, Jackson and I scour the ground, hunting for the perfect heart-shaped rock.

Some of our favourite rocks were that very first one from Brighton, one from a walk we took in the woods in Italy, just up the road from Degianno, and one we found on the rock beach in Clovelly. Some of the rocks need a bit more imaginative looking to see the heart shape, but these three are true heart rocks, and, for me and Jack, hearts ROCK!

Bubble Blowing

Brooke captures realistic looking "bubbles" that are guaranteed not to pop or splatter on her pages! Create "bubbles" by following the instructions on the following page. Double mat photos. Print journaling on light blue cardstock before using as second mat for photos. Print title, silhouette cut with craft knife. Randomly mount "bubbles" on pages as shown.

Brooke Smith, Anchorage, Alaska

Blowing

"Oh Mom look! Catch-A-Bubble! Can I get some PLEASE? I want the pink! Please Mom Please!?" I roll my eyes as Cheyenne runs up to the stand of orange, blue, green and pink bubble tubes. In the TV commercial, the bubbles magically all stick together and stack on top of each other creating mountains of shiny iridescent bubbles. "They don't pop!" booms the announcer. In reality, they are like a very weak plastic so they don't pop immediately, they kind of melt and leave behind a shiny sticky mess. I look down at Cheyenne and see the anxious excitement in her eyes and what else can I say? "Okay, you can get the pink."   August 2002

1 Draw circular shapes with crystal lacquer.

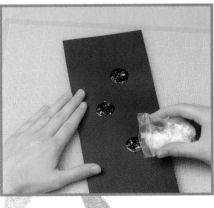

2 Sprinkle shaved ice into crystal lacquer circles.

3 Cover top of crystal lacquer circles with plastic watch crystal.

FALL

by Lois Duncan

Up from the meadow a wind is blowing,

The wind we longed for the summer through.

The sky, which was gold and hot and glowing,

Is high above us and strangely blue.

There, where the apple tree was budding

Ready to bloom, we hear a sound

And turn to find it's an apple thudding

Heavy and hard to the sunbaked ground.

A line of geese sweeps up from the river,

Dry leaves crunch on the browning lawn.

We look at each other, surprised, and shiver,

And suddenly—swiftly—summer is gone.

Autumn Pursuit

Unique stamped and embossed copper tags dangle on Heidi's rustic autumn layout. Double mat photos on solid-colored cardstocks; layer over textured patterned paper (source unknown). Print title and journaling on vellum and ivory cardstock. Silhouette cut title; mat on brown cardstock and silhouette cut again. Mount on page with self-adhesive foam spacers. Cut balance of title printed on cardstock to size, mat and mount on page with small copper brads. Paper tear journaling on vellum to size; mount under title. Stamp and emboss leaves (Hero Arts) onto light embossing copper (American Art Clay Co.). Cut into circles to fit tags (Avery). Tie with jute string; attach to first title letter. Create wheat stalk with colored raffia bunched together and tied with jute string. Attach copper tag designs to ends of jute string.

Heidi Schueller, Waukesha, Wisconsin

Autumn With Grandpa

Khristina collects memories of time spent with her grandfather like leaves on a lovely autumn day. Tear brown cardstock on all sides; brush edges with brown chalk and mount on tan cardstock. Brush brown chalk around edges of tan cardstock. Double and triple mat photos. Print title and poem on vellum, and journaling on tan cardstock. Paper tear edges around title and poem. Punch holes at top of title block; loop jute string through holes, tie in a knot and hang from twig. Mount twig with vellum attached on page over skeleton leaf (All Night Media). Mount poem over skeleton leaf on right-hand page. Freehand cut journaling into tag shape; mount leaf buttons (Jesse James) with glue dots and chalk around edges. Punch hole at top of tag and tie with fibers (On The Surface). Freehand cut smaller tags; punch hole and tie with fibers. Adhere leaf stickers (Mrs. Grossman's) over small patch of burlap mounted on tag.

Khristina Schuler, Oro Valley, Arizona

Chelsea

Gayla expresses adoration for her daughter with a sentimental quote embellished with soft fibers and colors. Print lines of text on white linen cardstock, leaving space to cut each line into rectangles. Cut to size; lightly rub brown chalk around edges. Adhere copper foil tape strip just under text. Attach large eyelets on each rectangle; weave fibers (Fibers by the Yard) through eyelets, linking pieces before mounting. Mat photo on mesh (Magenta) - covered cardstock. Cut four strips of copper foil tape; adhere diagonally at corners of photo; mount copper brad through all layers of matted photo. Mat again on torn patterned paper (Karen Foster Design) layered over a strip of mesh paper bordered with copper foil tape. Horizontally tear a 1½" strip of patterned paper; mount along bottom of page with small copper brads. Wrap page with fibers over paper-torn strip; attach copper tag (Anima Designs) with stamped name (Hero Arts) and date.

Gayla Feachen, Irving, Texas

Falling for Haley

Jodi builds a soft pile of punched leaves in warm autumn colors and a variety of textured papers. Print title on brown cardstock and journaling on tan cardstock. Cut title to size as a photo mat. Quadruple mat photo using title mat as third matting. Crop remaining photos; round corners and double mat. Round corners on first matting. Cut journaling to size; round corners and mat. Punch a variety of leaf shapes (Emagination Crafts, Hyglo/American Pin, Punch Bunch) from cardstock, vellum and mulberry papers in shades of brown and green. Cut a tan paper strip to form hill shape. Run through self adhesive machine. Place on page, sticky side up. Mount leaves to fill pile; randomly scatter a few leaves among photos.

Jodi Amidei, Memory Makers

Pumpkin Fest

Trudy adds an interesting dimensional surprise to her layout with a secret flip-up photo flap. Mat tan cardstock with dark brown cardstock for background. Horizontally tear 1" green cardstock strips; mount along bottom of page. Draw border lines on side and top edges with brown fine-tip pen. Paper piece pumpkins, scarecrow, birds and hay bales (Naptime Scrap); add dimension with pen and chalk. Wrap hay bales with wire. Mount pumpkins, hay bales and birds with self-adhesive foam spacers. Craft flip-up photo flap on right-hand page by matting two photos on orange cardstock. Mat together on one piece of brown cardstock. Score a horizontal line between the two photos; fold on scored line. Mount a third matted photo on cover flap. Mount flip-up photo flap on double-matted enlarged photo with self-adhesive foam spacers. Double mat photo for left page; mount over enlarged double matted photo. Print journaling on tan cardstock; cut and double mat. Detail title with orange and green chalks.

Trudy Sigurdson, Victoria, British Columbia, Canada

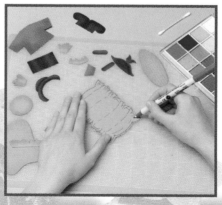

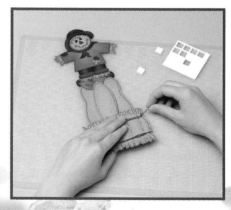

1 Cut out shapes using paper piecing patterns by Naptime Scrap. Use deckle-edged scissors for all straw pieces to create frayed look.

2 Chalk and do pen work to create outlines on paper pieces.

3 Assemble using self-adhesive foam spacers on pumpkin. Wire wrap to detail bale of hay.

Autumn

Copper-colored stamped and embossed foil leaves flutter among metallic fibers on Tammy's autumn-themed page. Double mat photos on brown and black cardstocks; layer on embossed copper-colored paper (K & Company). Print journaling on vellum and title letters on embossed cardstock (K & Company). Outline letters with gold gel pen; mat and silhouette cut. Trim journaling to size and mount on page with copper eyelets. Frame vellum with mounted metallic fibers as shown. Stamp leaves (Plaid) on copper colored foil paper (Embossing Arts); sprinkle with copper embossing powder. Set with heat gun. Silhouette cut shapes; layer atop metallic fibers. Mount title letters and leaf for letter "U" at top of page with self-adhesive foam spacers. Craft diamond-shaped foil embellishments by cutting long, thin triangles from foil paper. Roll "croissants"; randomly mount atop fibers.

Tammy Jackson, Spring Hill, Florida

Coloring Pumpkins

Textural cross-stitching with multi-stranded embroidery floss lends a homey feeling to Kristen's page. Slice two 2" strips of patterned paper (Scrap in a Snap); mount at top of orange cardstock background. Lightly draw two horizontal pencil lines; one on patterned paper strip and the other on background cardstock for guidelines; add ticking marks every ½". Pierce holes with needle at ticking marks; erase pencil lines. Stitch cross-stitch design. Print title and journaling on patterned paper. Cut to size and mount on page. Crop photos; mount over patterned paper squares layered on background cardstock. Cut preprinted image (EK Success); mat on patterned paper. Embellish title block with stitching as described above. Twist and curl silver wire to resemble image on die cut. Punch leaves (EK Success) from green cardstock; detail with pen and chalks before mounting atop wire.

Kristen Swain, Bear, Delaware

Some Mummy Loves You

Shannon has her page all "wrapped up" with a spooky textured background. Cut muslin strips; layer and mount on black cardstock. Triple mat photos on white and black cardstocks lightly brushed with black and white chalks. Print journaling on white cardstock; triple mat and brush with chalks. Write title on white cardstock; outline with black fine-tip pen. Mat on black cardstock and silhouette cut; mount at top of page. Complete page by randomly mounting plastic spiders.

Shannon Taylor, Bristol, Tennessee

Halloween 1992

Karen's diverse use of a variety of fibers adds color, texture and visual interest to her Halloween page. Mat gray cardstock with black cardstock. Slice two 1¾" strips of purple cardstock; horizontally mount four strands of colored fibers and attach on back of strip. Mat strip with black cardstock. Mount fibered strips at top and bottom of page. Die cut title letters (Sizzix); outline with black fine-tip pen before mounting on fibers. Punch bats from two-sided tape; cover with black glitter. Mount on title letters. Print journaling and date on white cardstock; cut to size and mat. Die cut ghosts and pumpkins (Sizzix); outline shapes with black fine-tip pen and detail with glitter. Mat photo on black cardstock; pierce small holes at corners and along sides of matting with needle. Stitch border with orange embroidery thread; mount on page. Hand draw haunted house, tree and moon on solid-colored paper and cut out. Outline tree and moon with black fine-tip pen; detail with chalk over pen lines. Mount yellow vellum behind haunted house windows. Layer images on matted brown cardstock. Freehand cut date into arrow shape; outline with black fine-tip pen and detail with chalk around edges. Pierce small holes at bottom of arrow and top of matted haunted house scene; stitch together with black embroidery thread.

Karen Cobb, Victoria, British Columbia, Canada

Vegan Thanksgiving

Lynne's comical approach to a vegan Thanksgiving is enhanced with colorful preprinted images and matching embellishments. Single and double mat photos on solid and patterned papers. Cut preprinted title and images (Kopp Design). Layer title block over mesh (Magic Mesh). Mount button images on mesh strip. Layer pie and metal frame (Anima Designs) on sliced strip of ivory cardstock detailed with black pen and brown chalk. Cut journal blocks from ivory cardstock; detail with pen and brown chalk. Stamp journaling quip with alphabet letters (Hero Arts). Tie threads on buttons; layer over punched rectangles, mesh and patterned paper pieces.

Lynne Rigazio Mau, Channahan, Illinois

Thanksgiving

Kristen builds on the distressed look of the autumn-themed stickers with paper-torn matting detailed and distressed with chalk and ink. Adhere border sticker strips (Karen Foster Design) at top of solid-colored cardstock. Cut two 3" strips of mesh (Magic Mesh); mount at bottom of pages. Double mat pumpkin stickers (Karen Foster Design) on brown and ivory cardstocks; paper tear all edges. Press edges of matting on brown inkpad and brush edges with brown chalk. Single and double mat photos; paper tear all edges of matting. Distress mattings in similar fashion as matted stickers. Print journaling on ivory cardstock; distress. Adhere pumpkin stickers at bottom of journaling block. Cut title letters with template (Scrap Pagerz) on ivory cardstock. Shade with burgundy chalk, blending from light to dark. Adhere leaf stickers on title.

Kristen Swain, Bear, Delaware

Fall Fun

Textured leaves playfully settle on decorative borders. Tear tan cardstock strip for horizontal border on left-hand page; brush with brown chalk on torn edges. Punch leaves (Marvy/Uchida) from colored cardstocks and lightweight copper mesh (American Art Clay Co). Crumple cardstock leaves; brush with brown chalk. Layer over curled wire along torn border. For vertical border on right-hand page, layer punched, textured and chalked leaves on tags adorned with copper eyelets and twine. Dry emboss leaf design (Darice) onto copper foil (MetalWorks) as shown below. Cut to size; layer over torn cardstock square before mounting on tag. Detail tags with chalk and pen before layering on page. Crop and slice segments into photos before matting on torn tags, cardstock and copper mesh. Detail photo tags and photo mats with pen outline. Add copper brads and wire to one photo mat. Cut title using template from green and brown cardstocks. Layer one word over dry-embossed leaf designs in copper foil. Mount over textured cardstock leaves on red torn cardstock strip; mat on tan cardstock. Outline second title word with black fine-tip pen.

Stacey Bohmer, Monroe, Michigan

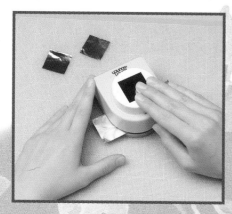

1 Punch out squares from light copper metal.

2 Using stylus, mouse pad and brass template; trace design into metal. Freehand draw veins and other details on each leaf.

3 Freehand draw a line around the square to add detail and dimension.

Cutest Li'l Pumpkins in the Patch

A dimensional paper-pieced pumpkin replaces a key word in the title of Gayla's fall layout. Double mat orange paper on patterned (Mustard Moon) and solid papers for background. Mat photos on orange paper; tear around edges. Adhere letter stickers (Colorbök) to scraps of orange paper with paper-torn edges. Slice slits in title blocks with craft knife; attach raffia and tie in a bow. Craft pumpkin with rolled patterned (Mustard Moon) paper strips. Slice strips of paper just longer than pumpkin shape about 1½" wide; roll tight and flatten with fingers. Mount on die-cut or freehand-drawn pumpkin shape; trim excess off around edges. Handcut stem from brown paper; brush brown chalk around edges of pumpkin for dimension. Mount wire leaf and vines (Crafts, Etc.) atop pumpkin before layering over raffia strips.

Gayla Feachen, Irving, Texas

4 Mount copper pieces on a torn square of brown cardstock and on top of a tag; detail with black pen, then add eyelet and jute.

Back to School

Holle photojournals her "back-to-school" rituals as a middle school teacher with freehand cut tags and vibrant embellishments that reflect her excitement for teaching. Mat photos on yellow cardstock; feature one photo by layering over red tinsel (Magic Scraps) and mesh paper (Magenta). Die cut title letters (Sizzix) from green corrugated cardstock; layer over mesh paper. Mount rhinestones in letter shapes to form word "to." Cut balance of title letters with template (Wordsworth) from blue cardstock; set aside. Print journaling and photo captions for tags on green cardstock. Cut journaling block to size; layer with template title words and mount on page. Freehand cut tag shapes around photo text; mount star eyelet (Making Memories) and tie with yarn. Mount on photos with self-adhesive foam spacers.

Holle Wiktorek, Clarksville, Tennessee

Backpack to School

Diana makes the grade with clever refurbishing of an old backpack strap that sets the tone for a first-day-of-school page. Slice a 2¼" strip of green paper and a ¼" strip of white cardstock; mount on dark green cardstock near bottom of page. Take apart strap of an old backpack; remove spongy material inside strap. Fold and cut blue cardstock over spongy material to resemble strap; attach buckle and stitch design with sewing machine. Mount down left side of page with glue dots. Print journaling on green cardstock, leaving room for photo. Layer photo on cut journaling block; mount on page with small black brads. Punch small photo squares; layer with mesh (Magic Mesh) on journaling block. Freehand cut tag; machine stitch white title block to tag. Layer mesh pieces and stitch letter charm on tag with embroidery thread. Punch hole at top of tag; secure black ribbon through hole to back of tag. Write balance of title and photo captions on green cardstock scraps with black marker; mount on title block with black brad.

Diana Hudson, Bakersfield, California
Photos, Ramona Payne, Henderson, Nevada

Are You Ready for Some Football

Kelli's textured football shape, laced and layered, begs an answer to the famous Monday Night question "Are you ready for some football?" Single and double mat photos on red and yellow cardstocks. Print partial title; cut to size and mat. Mount on page with self-adhesive foam spacers. Die cut (Accu-Cut) balance of title letters from textured paper; mat on white cardstock and silhouette cut. Freehand cut football shape from textured paper. Paint stripes with acrylic paints. Freehand cut stitched and laced area for football. Punch holes for laces; weave shoelace horizontally and vertically. Mount on football shape with self-adhesive foam spacers. Cut journal block to curve around football; mat with red cardstock and write with black fine-tip pen.

Kelli Noto, Centennial, Colorado

Yom Kippur

Debbie takes a solemn approach to the holiest of all Jewish holidays with dramatic layers of black cardstock detailed with colored chalks and torn mulberry paper (Stampin' Up!). Tear black cardstock on all edges; brush colored chalks with a heavy hand on torn edges in shades of blue, green and yellow. Mount on white cardstock background; write words to holiday song around edges as a border. Mat photos; mount on black cardstock layered over torn green mulberry paper. Print title and journaling on vellum. Tear printed vellum into strips; mount title strip at top of page over yellow cardstock strip with small brads. Stamp Star of David on journaling blocks; sprinkle with embossing powder and set with heat embossing gun. Color title words and embossed star with blue, green and yellow colored pencils. Mount journaling strip in same fashion as title strip.

Debbie DeMars, Overland Park, Kansas

Madeleine Walters

Mary Anne tells a delightful story with an intriguing fold-out design that opens up to display pop-up photo tags. Slice two 6" wide strips of tan cardstock and two 4" strips of brown patterned paper (Faux Memories); score with bone folder. Start accordion fold at 1" toward inside of paper; fold back and forth at ½" intervals four times, leaving a 1" end on each side. Crop photos into tags; mount on cardstock. Punch ½" circles, mount at end of tag. Punch hole through circle layered on photo; tie fibers (Memory Crafts). Mount photo tags at center of accordion fold; reinforce by mounting a ⅜ x 4" strip cut from brown patterned paper. Mount around ends of center fold. Mount ends of "hinge" on page and flap. Cover "hinge" flaps with a 12 x 12" sheet of green patterned paper (Scrap-Ease). Print journaling on green patterned paper; cut 6" wide. Mount 6" journaling strip on inside flap, covering "hinge" flap. Triple mount enlarged photo on solid and patterned papers. Print title and journaling on brown patterned paper; cut to size and mat on yellow cardstock. Mount enlarged matted photo and title/journaling blocks. Stitch buttons to top and bottom inner edges with embroidery thread. Reinforce sewn buttons with two ½" punched circles layered under and over journaled paper. Pierce holes through layers before stitching. Mount 6" journaled strip with buttons. Tie 4½" piece of embroidery thread, embellished with beads, around buttons on left flap. Fold flaps toward inside; close and secure.

Mary Anne Walters, Monk Sherborne, Tadley, UK

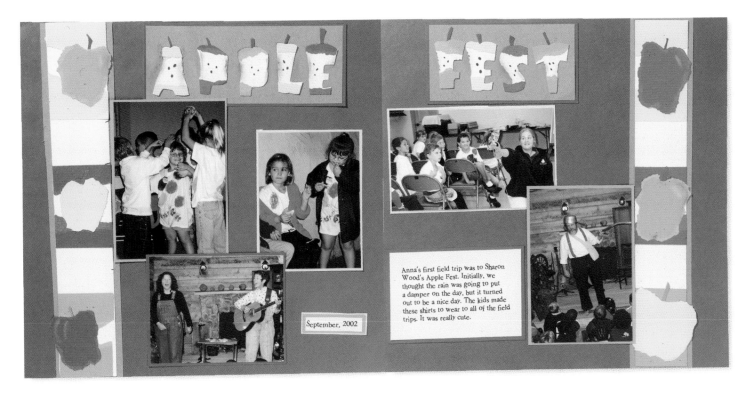

Apple Fest

Mary Faith cleverly modified and detailed template-cut title letters for her page to reflect the theme of her photos. Slice two 2¼" tan and two 1¾" cream strips of cardstock for vertical borders. Adhere cream strip to tan strip. Horizontally layer small sliced and torn strips of red, yellow and green cardstocks to cream strip border. Paper tear apple shapes from colored cardstocks; layer on border with cut "stems." Mat photos. Print journaling; cut to size and mat. Create title letters as shown on right and below.

Mary Faith Roell, Harrison, Ohio
Crystal Heyob, Harrison, Ohio

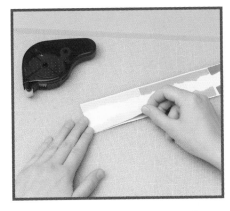

1 Tear strips of yellow, green and red cardstock; mount on 2" strip of cream cardstock.

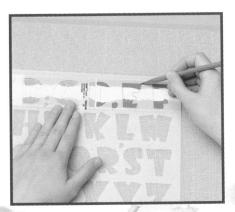

2 Using template (Scrap Pagerz), trace letters onto previously prepared strip of cream and colored cardstocks. Alternate color of letters throughout title.

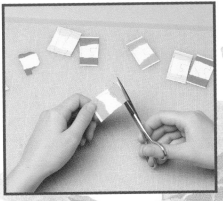

3 Cut out letters. Create "bite marks" by allowing scissors to form an irregular pattern in the center of each apple letter.

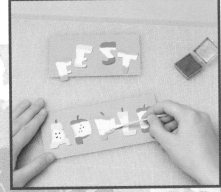

4 Freehand cut apple stems; adhere. Add brown chalk to "bite mark" edges and draw in "seeds" using brown marker. Cut title block from tan cardstock; mount on red and adhere letters.

Fresh corn. One of summer's sweetest treats! Thanks to Meredith, corn-on-the-cob will forever be known as corn-on-the-bone in the Rife family. To her four year old mind, this name makes a lot more sense. She started calling it that the first time we had fresh corn this summer. The name stuck. Our favorite lazy summer days end with a cook-out on the deck. Lindsay and Meredith shuck the corn, and Daddy cooks on the grill. After a yummy meal of steaks and corn-on-the-bone, we all catch lightning bugs in the backyard. Even during the cold days of winter, eating corn-on-the-bone will bring back memories of these lazy summer days. (2002)

Corn on the Bone

Jane takes paper yarn to new heights with a cleverly fashioned corn cob and title letters. Triple mat photos on patterned (Colorbök) and solid-colored papers. Print journaling on yellow cardstock; cut to size and outline shape with green fine-tip pen. Cut title letters from flattened paper yarn (Making Memories); mount on yellow cardstock. Add green pen-line details. Attach triangle eyelets (Happy Hammer) to page at corners around title block; frame with paper yarn. Weave through eyelets and secure to back of page. Craft corn cob out of flattened paper yarn; cut husk shapes from green paper yarn. Layer with yellow flattened paper yarn pieces rolled into balls. Slice thin strips of yellow paper yarn for corn "hairs"; shade ends with brown chalk. Attach eyelets over solid and patterned paper squares; randomly attach eyelets.

Jane Rife, Hendersonville, Tennessee

The Corn Maze

Trudy's page is bordered with colorful torn-paper corn stalks. Slice two 5½" strips of brown cardstock. Slice three 1 x 4" strips to attach flap to page. Horizontally mount sliced strips to back of flap and back of page. Attach eyelets to remaining 5½" cardstock strip. Weave jute string through eyelets in cross-cross fashion; attach string at back. Mount strip with eyelets and string to back of flap. Tear ½"-¾" strips of green cardstock; mount around edges of page and flap for border. Tear small pieces of green cardstock; layer with yellow torn cardstock. Mount layered torn pieces at upper right-hand corner. Mat photos on brown cardstock; slice one and mount on page. Cut three pieces of brown cardstock, each 4¼ x 6⅝". Mount photos on front and back of cardstock, leaving a ½" space at top. Mount one photo on third piece of cardstock; layer pieces together. Mount eyelets at top of first photo flap, 1" in from each side of cardstock. Punch two holes at top of second and third piece. Loop jute string through each layer's punched holes; tie together. Mount on page with strong adhesive. Print partial title and journaling on tan cardstock; cut to size and mount on brown cardstock. Cut remaining title letters with template (Frances Meyer) from yellow cardstock layered with dark yellow and green paper strips. Mat on brown cardstock and silhouette cut; mount on title block. Mount journaling block on outside of flap under jute string. Slip brochure under jute strings over journaling.

Trudy Sigurdson, Victoria, British Columbia, Canada

BEGINNING AGAIN

by Lois Duncan

The close of a year is a milestone.
We find it both painful and sweet.
A dawn has evolved into sunset,
A chapter of life is complete.

Its wonders are now only memories,
And all of the stories are told.
Tomorrow's adventures lie waiting
With new sagas yet to unfold.

Although we are glad to move onward,
The past is an intricate part.
Its memories, like beautiful music,
Were strummed on the strings of the heart.

So cherish those wonderful memories.
Hold them and cuddle them tight,
Then tuck them away in a scrapbook
And bid them a tender goodnight.

Additional Instructions and Credits

The Noto Family, *cover*

Randomly emboss, stamp and add gold leaf to six sheets of coordinating cardstock. When finished, rip or cut papers into smaller pieces. On a sheet of 8½ x 11" paper, adhere pieces, overlapping, to create a collage. Use a tag-shaped template (Accu-Cut) to cut four tags. Punch multiple leaves (Family Treasures) from collaged paper. Cut photo frame from remaining portion of collaged paper. Double mat photo on white and burgundy cardstock before mounting on frame. Rip border; apply liquid glue to edges. When dried to tacky, press on gold leaf, removing excess when dry. Use block template to create title (Provo Craft) and a stencil to create journaling. Apply liquid glue to drawn stenciled letters and press on gold leaf. Mount "Fall" title letters on tags with self adhesive foam spacers. Add fibers to tags by tying through small punched holes set with eyelets.

Jodi Amidei, Memory Makers
Photo, Kelli Noto, Centennial, Colorado

Snow, *page 6*

Crumple white cardstock for texture; flatten and mat with dark blue cardstock. Lightly adhere mosaic overlay (DieCuts with a View) onto white textured background. Stamp large and small snowflakes (Duncan) with lavender and blue ink onto background. Dust lightly with blue and lavender chalk. Gently remove overlay. Double and triple mat smaller photos. Quadruple mat larger photo; paper tear bottom edges of last two mats. Stamp title letters with lavender ink onto white paper; silhouette cut and mount on double-matted white square with self-adhesive foam spacers. Write journaling and mat. Stamp snowflake shapes on white cardstock; silhouette-cut using scissors and craft knife for small details. Add glitter glue on title words and snowflakes. Mount silhouette-cut snowflakes with self-adhesive foam spacers.

Jodi Amidei, Memory Makers
Photos, Michele Gerbrandt, Memory Makers

Spring, *page 9*

Assemble torn, patterned papers (Magenta) atop torn, solid paper strip to form background. Punch jumbo, large, medium and small squares (Emagination Crafts, Family Treasures, Punch Bunch) from complementary-colored cardstock and patterned papers (Magenta). Repunch squares with giant, jumbo, large and medium square punches to create the square frames. Arrange and adhere square frames randomly across lower page border, allowing corners to overlap playfully and using self-adhesive foam spacers occasionally for lift. Create framed, vertical title block with cardstock, foam tape for lift and letter stickers (ChYops/Mercer Motifs) over patterned paper; mount on side of page. Add triple-matted photos and journaling block. Finish page with floral sticker accents (EK Success) rubbed with chalk at photo, and title block corners and in square frames on lower page border.

Jodi Amidei, Memory Makers
Photos, Gloria Hart, Winter Haven, Florida

Glossary of Scrapbook Terms and Techniques

Acid-Free

Look for scrapbook products—particularly pages, paper, adhesives and inks—that are free from harmful acids that can eat away at the emulsion of your photos.

Archival Quality

A nontechnical term suggesting that a substance is chemically stable, durable and permanent and is safe to use alongside photos.

Buffered Paper

Paper in which certain alkaline substances have been added during the manufacturing process to prevent acids from forming in the future due to chemical reactions.

Embellishments

Page accents you can make or buy. Can include stickers, die cuts, stamped images, punch art, beads, buttons, rhinestones, sequins, pens, chalks, charms, wire, ribbon, embroidery floss, and thread.

Journaling

Refers to handwritten, handmade or computer-generated text that provides pertinent details about what is taking place in photographs.

Lignin-Free

Paper products that are void of the material (sap) that holds wood fibers together as a tree grows. Most paper is lignin-free except for newsprint, which yellows and becomes brittle with age.

Memorabilia

Mementos and souvenirs saved from travel, school and life's special events—things that are worthy of remembrance.

Page Protectors

Plastic sleeves or pockets that encase finished scrapbook pages for protection. Use only PVC-free protectors.

Pigment Ink

Pigment inks are water-insoluble and do not penetrate the page surface. Instead, they adhere to the paper, providing better contrast and sharpness.

PVC or Polyvinyl Chloride

A plastic that should not be used in a scrapbook, it emits gases, which cause damage to photos. Use only PVC-free plastic page protectors and memorabilia. Safe plastics include polypropylene, polyethylene, and polyester or Mylar.

Patterns

Use these patterns to complete scrapbook pages featured in this book. All patterns are shown at fifty percent. Use a photocopier to enlarge patterns before transferring them to your paper.

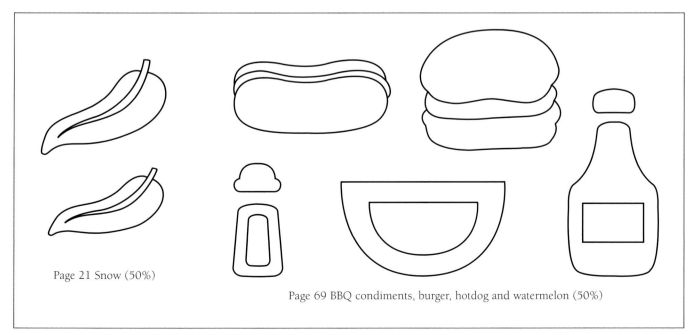

Page 21 Snow (50%)

Page 69 BBQ condiments, burger, hotdog and watermelon (50%)

Credits and Sources

The following Memory Makers Masters have contributed their talents and artwork to the creation of this book:

Valerie Barton, Brandi Ginn, Diana Graham, Diana Hudson, Torrey Miller, Kelli Noto, Heidi Schueller, Trudy Sigurdson, Holle Wiktorek

The following companies manufacture products showcased on scrapbook pages within this book. Please check your local retailers to find these materials. We have made every attempt to properly credit the items mentioned in this book and apologize to those we may have missed.

3M Stationery
(800) 364-3577
www.3M.com

Accu-Cut®
(800) 288-1670
www.accucut.com

All Night Media®, Inc.
(800) 782-6733
www.allnightmedia.com

American Art Clay Co., Inc.
(800) 374-1600
www.amaco.com

Anima Designs
(800) 570-6847
www.animadesigns.com

Art Accents, Inc.
(360) 733-8989
www.artaccents.net

Autumn Leaves
(800) 588-6707 (wholesale only)

Avery Dennison Corporation
(800) 462-8379
www.avery.com

Bazzill Basics Paper
(480) 558-8557

Beadery®, The
(401) 539-2432

Broderbund Software
(319) 247-3325
www.broderbund.com

Carolee's Creations™
(463) 563-1100 (wholesale only)
www.carolees.com

Charming Pages
(888) 889-5060

Close To My Heart®
(888) 655-6552
www.closetomyheart.com

Club Scrap™, Inc.
(888) 634-9100
www.clubscrap.com

C.M. Offray & Son, Inc.
www.offray.com

Colorbök
(800) 366-4660 (wholesale only)
www.colorbok.com

Coronado Island Stamping
(619) 477-8900
www.cistamping.com

Crafter's Workshop, The
(877) CRAFTER
www.thecraftersworkshop.com

Crafts, Etc. Ltd.
(800) 888-0321
www.craftsetc.com

Creative Imaginations
(800) 942-6487
www.cigift.com

Creative Memories®
(800) 468-9335
www.creative-memories.com

C-Thru® Ruler Company, The
(800) 243-8419 (wholesale only)
www.cthruruler.com

Cut-It-Up™
(530) 389-2233
www.scrapamento.com

Darice, Inc.
(800) 321-1494
www.darice.com

Debbie Mumm®
(888) 819-2923
www.debbiemumm.com

Deluxe Cuts
(480) 497-9005
www.deluxecuts.com

Design Originals
(800) 877-7820
www.d-originals.com

DieCuts with a View™
(877) 221-6107

DMC Corp.
(973) 589-0606
www.dmc.com

DMD Industries, Inc.
(800) 805-9890 (wholesale only)
www.dmdind.com

Doodlebug Design, Inc.™
(801) 966-9952

Duncan Enterprises
(559) 294-3282
www.duncan-enterprises.com

EK Success™ Ltd.
(800) 524-1349 (wholesale only)
www.eksuccess.com

Ellison® Craft and Design
(800) 253-2238
www.ellison.com

Emagination Crafts, Inc.
(630) 833-9521
ww.emaginationcrafts.com

Embossing Arts Company
(800) 662-7955
www.embossingarts.com

EZ2Cut Templates
(260) 489-9212
www.ez2cut.com

Family Treasures, Inc.®
(800) 413-2645
www.familytreasures.com

Faux Memories
(813) 269-7946
www.fauxmemories.com

Fibers by the Yard
www.fibersbytheyard.com

Fiskars, Inc.
(800) 950-0203
www.fiskars.com

Frances Meyer, Inc.®
(800) 372-6237
www.francesmeyer.com

Happy Hammer, The
(303) 690-3883 (wholesale only)
www.thehappyhammer.com

Hasbro
www.hasbro.com

Hero Arts® Rubber Stamps, Inc.
(800) 822-4376 (wholesale only)
www.heroarts.com

Hot Off The Press, Inc.
(800) 227-9595
www.paperpizazz.com

Hyglo®/American Pin
(800) 821-7125 (wholesale only)
www.american-pin.com

Ivy Cottage
(888) 303-1375
www.ivycottagecreations.com

Jesse James & Co., Inc.
(610) 435-0201
www.jessejamesbutton.com

JewelCraft, LLC
(201) 223-0804
www.jewelcraft.biz

Jewish Stickers, L.L.C.
www.jewishstickers.com

JHB International
(303) 751-8100
www.buttons.com

JudiKins
(310) 515-1115

K & Company
(888) 244-2083 (wholesale only)
www.kandcompany.com

Karen Foster Design
(801) 451-9779
www.karenfosterdesign.com

Keeping Memories Alive®
(800) 419-4949
www.scrapbooks.com

Kopp Design
(208) 656-0734
www.koppdesign.com

Magenta Rubber Stamps
(800) 565-5254
www.magentarubberstamps.com

Magic Mesh™
(651) 345-6374
www.magicmesh.com

Magic Scraps™
(972) 385-1838
www.magicscraps.com

Making Memories
(800) 286-5263
www.makingmemories.com

Mark Enterprises/Stampendous®
(800) 869-0474
www.stampendous.com

Marvy® Uchida
(800) 541-5877
www.uchida.com

Masterpiece® Studios
(800) 447-0219
www.masterpiecestudios.com

McGill, Inc.
(800) 982-9884
www.mcgillinc.com

Memory Crafts
www.memorycrafts.com

Mercer Motifs, Inc./ CHYOPS
(801) 205-3268

MetalWorks - no contact info. available

Mrs. Grossman's Paper Company
(800) 429-4549 (wholesale only)
www.mrsgrossmans.com

Mustard Moon™ Paper Co.
(408) 229-8542
www.mustardmoon.com

Naptime Scrap™
(816) 584-1274

On The Fringe
www.onthefringe.net

On The Surface
(847) 675-2520

Pakon, Inc.
(866) 227-1229
www.pakon.com

Paper Adventures®
(800) 727-0699 (wholesale only)
www.paperadventures.com

Paper Company, The
(800) 426-8989

Paper Fever, Inc.
(801) 412-0495
www.paperfever.com

Paper Garden, The
(210) 494-9602
www.papergarden.com

Paper House Productions
(800) 255-7316
www.paperhouseproductions.com

Pioneer Photo Albums®
(800) 366-3686
www.pioneerphotoalbums.com

Plaid Enterprises
(800) 842-4197
www.plaidonline.com

PrintWorks
(800) 854-6558

Provo Craft®
(888) 577-3545 (wholesale only)
www.provocraft.com

PSX Design™
(800) 782-6748
www.psxdesign.com

Pulsar Paper Products
(877) 861-0031

Punch Bunch, The
(254) 791-4209
www.thepunchbunch.com

Ranger Industries, Inc.
(800) 244-2211

Sakura Hobby Craft
(310) 212-7878

Sandylion Sticker Designs
(800) 387-4215
www.sandylion.com

Sanford® Corp.
(800) 323-0749
www.sanfordcorp.com

Scrapbook Sally
(435) 645-0696
www.scrapbooksally.com

Scrap-Ease®
(800) 642-6762
www.whatsnewltd.com

Scrap in a Snap™
(866) 462-7627
www.scrapinasnap.com

Scrap Pagerz
(425) 645-0696
www.scrappagerz.com

Scrappin' Dreams
(417) 831-1882 (wholesale only)
www.scrappindreams.com

Scrapyard 329
(775) 829-1118
www.scrapyard329.com

SEI, Inc.
(800) 333-3279
www.nagposh.com

Sizzix
(866) 742-4447
www.sizzix.com

Stampa Rosa, Inc.
(800) 554-5755
www.stamparosa.com

Stamp Barn, The
(800) 246-1142
www.stampbarn.com

Stamp Doctor, The
www.stampdoctor.com

Stampin' Up!®
(800) 782-6787
www.stampinup.com

Stampscapes™
(714) 968-5541
www.stampscapes.com

Stickopotamus®
(888) 270-4443 (wholesale only)
www.stickopotamus.com

Suze Weinberg Design Studio
(732) 761-2410
www.schmoozewithsuze.com

Sweetwater
(800) 359-3094
www.sweetwaterscrapbook.com

This n' That Crafts
(860) 485-1788
www.easymats.com

Tsukineko®, Inc.
(800) 769-6633
www.tsukineko.com

Two Busy Moms
(800) 272-4794
www.twobusymoms.com

Westrim® Crafts
(800) 727-2727 (wholesale only)
www.westrimcrafts.com

Wordsworth
(719) 282-3495
www.wordsworthstamps.com

Index